Living in the U.S.A.
Fifth Edition

Alison R. Lanier

Revised by Charles William Gay

INTERCULTURAL PRESS, INC.

Intercultural Press, Inc.
P.O. Box 700
Yarmouth, Maine 04096 USA
207-846-5168

Originally published 1973 by Charles Scribner's Sons
Published 1978, 1981, 1988, 1996 by Intercultural Press

Book design and production by Patty J. Topel
Cover design and production by Patty J. Topel

Printed in the United States of America

03   02   01   00   99   98   4   5   6   7   8   9

Library of Congress Cataloging-in-Publication Data

Lanier, Alison Raymond.
    Living in the U.S.A. / Alison R. Lanier: revised by Charles William Gay.—5th ed.
        p.   cm.
    Originally published: New York: Charles Scribner's Sons, 1973.
    Includes index.
    ISBN 1-877864-40-4
    1. United States—Social life and customs—1971-. 2. United States—Guidebooks.   I. Gay, Charles William. II. Title.

E169.02.L26 1996
973.92'9—dc20   95—53161
                                                        CIP

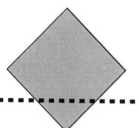

Table of Contents

Appendices

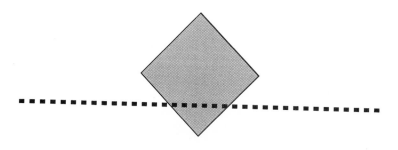

Preface to the Fifth Edition

Welcome to a country that is never what you think it is. Because of the great diversity among people, geography, and climate, you can read before you visit this country, you can talk to people from your country about their experiences here, you can even talk to Americans who are visiting your country, but still you can never be quite sure what you will find when you arrive. It is part of the excitement of this land of many faces. We welcome millions of visitors and new residents every year, and we know that they will sometimes be overwhelmed by what they find.

If Alison R. Lanier were still living, she would no doubt have revised the book herself. Most of this fifth edition retains her insight into what visitors need to know, and her verve and humor still come through. But things change fast in this country; thus, this edition contains new statistics and insights and, I trust, some indication of my own feelings and attitudes about my country.

I returned not long ago from a wonderful ten years' living in Japan. There I taught English to Japanese students, taught teachers about teaching English to speakers of other languages, and taught intercultural communication to Japanese graduate students and to graduate students from other countries who were residents in Japan. Before that I spent many years teaching foreign students from around the world at the University of Southern California. I hope this book provides the sort of information hundreds of these students have asked me about over the years.

I also hope that this new edition helps thousands of visitors to this country, just as the earlier editions did. In spite of the great diversity in the United States, there are some guidelines which can be very helpful for visitors to know when they first arrive. This book is an attempt to provide some of that basic information.

Charles William Gay

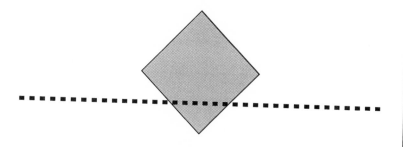

Original Preface

This book stems from conversations with countless people from all over the world. I am grateful for their thoughtful contributions to it.

The book was first published in 1973 by Charles Scribner's Sons. Since then it has been revised, updated, and republished in many paperback editions. It has also been published in nine other countries and seven languages.

The book grew out of the experiences of my own firm, Overseas Briefing Associates, which worked for many years with U.S. and foreign personnel, helping them adjust to unfamiliar countries and conditions.

I hope this guide to American life will ease your path and help you to understand the vast land and varied people that make up these United States.

Alison R. Lanier

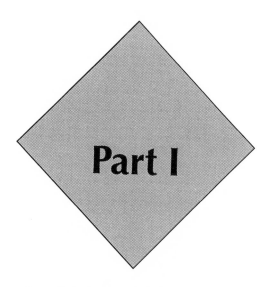

Part I

American Intangibles

1

First Impressions

Relocation to the United States is frequently a difficult transition, even though a chance to live in a different culture is an exciting prospect for most people. Newcomers have many questions: Where will we live? Where can we find household help? How difficult is it to buy a car? What kinds of taxes must be paid and when? What customs and courtesies are different? What medical services are available? The list seems almost endless.

It is easier than ever to move from one place to another in this age of jet travel. Instant broadcast news bounced off satellites enables us to view each other more and more clearly from the comfort of our homes all around the world. Such developments have led to increasing interaction among nations, and with this comes the transfer of diplomats, businesspeople, executives, and students—often accompanied by spouses and families.

Pace

The first impression visitors have of the United States is usually in one of the major cities, since most jets land in Boston, New York, Miami, Washington, D.C., Los Angeles, San Francisco, Seattle, Dallas, Atlanta, or Chicago. In these metropolises the pace of life is fast. People are in a rush to get where they are going, waiting impatiently to be served a meal, restlessly seeking attention in a store, bumping into other people as they walk fast along the street. Bus drivers and taxi drivers may not seem friendly, waiters may hurry you, department store salespeople may not spend much time with you. You may not see many smiles, it may be difficult to have a conversation with strangers, you may get lost in the crowds. All this can be frightening and confusing unless you are accustomed to city life in your own country. Don't take such behavior personally; this is life in the city. The pace is more gentle outside the big cities, as it is in other countries.

Americans who live in cities assume that everyone is in a hurry and is self-sufficient and that people know where they are going and how to get there, just as city people do in Tokyo or Paris, in Cairo or São Paulo. If you need assistance or want to ask a question, people who work in hotels, department stores, restaurants, shops, and many other places will usually help you if you ask them in a friendly manner. Friendliness will almost always be returned. *But you must let them know that you need help;* otherwise, they will not notice you because they are thinking about their own concerns. A few may not respond helpfully. If this happens, don't be discouraged; just ask someone else. Most Americans enjoy helping a stranger.

People

Who are these people who are swirling around you? Of the 255 million or so that call the United States home, most have their origins in other parts of the world. The names you see over shop doors tell you so, as do the varied types of faces you pass on the streets. A roll call of schoolchildren will include such names as Adams, Ali, Bykowski, Capparella, Fujita, Gonzales, Mukerji, Nusseibeh, and Wong. Mostly, these diverse backgrounds have not been blended in the so-called American "melting pot." In fact, the idea that the United States is a melting pot is largely a myth. Instead, most ethnic groups retain many of their own customs and social traditions. They merge into the American mainstream only in certain aspects of life—in schools, sports, business, and science, to name a few—but keep to many of their own cultural patterns socially and in their homes.

There is currently considerable discussion as to how much bilingualism—primarily English and Spanish—should be allowed or encouraged in schools, government documents, and election ballots. Many such tensions now apparent in American life originate from the interaction of varied cultures. The plus side of this situation is the richness that comes with variety, the wide freedom of choice that exists in ideas and dress, in food and in customs. The minus side is that unseen barriers do still exist for some people. For example, business or professional advancement may be difficult, and adequate housing may be hard to find—especially at lower income levels. Nonetheless, everyone can find his or her own familiar world here—be it in spices or fruits, churches or national groups, newspapers or music.

Informality

Although American informality is well known, many interpret it as a lack of respect when they first encounter it, especially in the business world. The almost immediate use of first names, for example, may be a shock to those long accustomed to being status conscious, since the use of first names in some cultures signals a fair degree of intimacy.

Don't be surprised if Americans do not shake hands, especially in informal situations. They often just nod or smile instead. A casual "Hi" or "How are you doing?" or "Hello" often takes the place of a formal handshake, but it means the same thing. Nor will you find Americans circulating among fellow office workers or people at a party giving each one a personal farewell. Instead—again the different sense of timing and pace—they will just wave a cheery "good-bye" or say something informal to the whole group, such as "Well, see you tomorrow" or "So long everybody." Then they will leave. No handshakes.

You will see even high-level executives working at office desks in shirtsleeves, sometimes without their ties. They may lean far back in their chairs and even put their feet on the desk while they talk on the telephone. This is not meant to be rude. Once we get out of the tense, hurried city streets, we are an informal people.

Our pace is often either totally hurried, intense, work-absorbed, and competitive (in play as well as work) or else totally at ease and informal, a relaxed manner described as "laid-back." We tend to swing between these extremes. This is the pendulum you need to understand if you are to understand the United States and its people.

Size

It is difficult to really experience or "feel" the size of the United States, even when you know the actual number of miles from coast to coast. To get the full impact you should realize, for example, that it takes forty-eight hours (two entire days and two long nights) to travel by train from Chicago to Los Angeles, rolling along hour after hour across wheat fields, mountains, and deserts; Chicago is an overnight train trip from New York.

Another way to think about it is to compare distances in the United States with others more familiar to you. For example, New York to Washington, D.C. is about the same as London to Paris or Nairobi to Mombasa or Tokyo to Kyoto; New York to Los Angeles is farther than Lisbon to Cairo or Moscow to Montreal or New Delhi to Rome.

It is difficult for those people who come from smaller countries to realize how important this matter of size is in the lives of Americans. Not only is the country vast, it also contains 255 million people. These two factors affect every phase of life, not only creating a highly competitive domestic market for goods, which gives rise to constant advertising, but also causing an equally competitive political arena. Wide geographic differences make for profound differences in attitudes and values. A New Englander, for example, is often quite different in point of view from a Texan, and a Hawaiian may not understand the values of a Minnesotan. Marked differences in geography or weather and widely dispersed ethnic heritages naturally affect people's attitudes—but in the

United States such differences occur within the same nation. An overseas visitor once remarked, "No wonder Americans talk so loud and move so fast. In a place that size you almost have to or you get lost in the shuffle."

Time Zones

Another way to comprehend the vastness of the country's size is to be aware of the time changes. There are four different time zones between the two coasts. When it is 12:00 noon Eastern Standard Time in New York, it is 11:00 A.M. Central Standard Time in Chicago, 10:00 A.M. Mountain Standard Time in Denver, and 9:00 A.M. Pacific Standard Time in San Francisco.

Canada, being wider from east to west, adds one more time zone: Atlantic Standard Time for New Brunswick, Nova Scotia, Newfoundland, and Labrador. Alaska (the forty-ninth state of the United States, but not adjoining) extends even farther west than Canada and adds an additional two time zones, Alaska Standard Time and Nome Standard Time. Hawaii (the fiftieth state) is a group of islands in the Pacific Ocean, about 2,400 miles west of the U.S. mainland. Since it is directly south of Alaska, it uses Alaska Standard Time. The American continent is so wide that it encompasses *one-third* of all the world's time zones.

The world's date line is halfway around the world from Zero Meridian, that is, twelve hours away from Greenwich, on the 180th Meridian. Luckily for all of us, the line runs for the most part through the open Pacific—the most convenient spot it could be! East of this imaginary line, the calendar is a day earlier than points west of it. People coming to the United States from Asia will therefore add a day to their lives—until they go home again!

Climate

Naturally, with such distances, the climate in the continental United States is also one of great extremes. From New England and New York through Chicago and much of the Midwest and

Northwest, temperatures vary from subzero in winter to the high nineties or over in summer (Fahrenheit).

The South and the Southwest have warmer weather, though even these sections have occasional frosts and periods of moderate cold. Generally, summers are likely to range from 70°F to 100°F (21°C to 38°C), and many areas can be quite humid. However, air conditioning is so widespread that you can expect most buildings—even many private homes—to be kept at relatively comfortable temperatures.

Alaskan temperatures are, of course, extremely cold most of the year, while Hawaii enjoys a very moderate climate. Temperatures there are normally in the seventies and eighties (Fahrenheit).

2

Customs Vary with Cultures

Many American customs will surprise you; the same thing happens to us when we visit another country. People living in various cultures handle many small daily activities differently. Some differences are minor, and one soon becomes accustomed to them. At first, for example, people may find the transitory quality of much of American life odd—the fact, for example, that one can rent art by the week or the entire furnishings of an apartment, from sofa and beds to the last spoon, on less than eight hours' notice. Supermarkets offer a wide variety of packaged foods that busy people can prepare quickly so that they can spend more time in recreational activities than in domestic chores. Large chain stores located in huge warehouses offer discount prices for goods sold in bulk packaging. "Packaged" living is part of today's American scene, part of its mobility and pace.

At the same time—and perhaps even *because* of a sense of impermanence—houses interest Americans greatly. They spend much time thinking and reading and talking about the design of houses, their decorations, how to improve them. Many weekend hours are passed in "do-it-yourself" projects around the house. People also love to look at each other's houses. Since they would thoroughly enjoy visiting and examining a house in another country, they assume that you will probably have the same desire. Don't be surprised, therefore, if you are shown the entire house from top to bottom, including bathrooms and closets! Don't make the mistake of refusing; the whole house may have been cleaned especially for you!

Because our people have come from so many nationalities, there is a far wider range of what is acceptable than in some countries where the inhabitants have grown up with a common heritage. As a result, no one needs to feel awkward or uncomfortable in following his or her own customs. Although Americans are noticeably informal, if you prefer somewhat greater formality, feel free to act in your own way. This will be acceptable to those around you. You can "do your own thing" and be respected here to a very large extent.

However, it may help to have a little guidance in understanding some general customs in the United States. The subject is, of course, too broad and the ethnic differences too great to cover fully, but the following are a few common patterns you may encounter.

Personal Questions

Conversational questions may seem to you both too personal and too numerous—especially when you first arrive. "Where do you work?" "Are you married?" "How many children do you have?" "Do you play golf? What is your score?" These are not personal questions by American standards. They are a search for common ground on which to build a relationship or base a conversation. Such questions are meant to be friendly; the questioner is interested in you and is not prying into your private life, at least not deliberately. What is considered personal varies across cultures.

This is the way in which we become acquainted with one another. Since many of us move around the country so often and meet so many people in the course of a year, we tend to make quick assessments of each other. We meet, and by rapid questioning we decide whether we wish to establish a relationship, for we know that in this fluid society we don't have time to learn about each other more slowly.

In less mobile countries people operate on a different basis. They protect their privacy and their position at first, and hold off any moves toward intimacy until there has been adequate time to assess the newcomer. Only then do they feel comfortable in discussing anything as personal as their children, or where they live, or what they do at work. The difference is more of timing than of intent. Americans move faster, living like a movie that is run at double speed, because tomorrow they may be transferred across the country or you may go back across the sea.

To those coming from countries where introductory amenities are normally handled more slowly and over a longer period of time, the American way can seem threatening in its personal intensity; yet, even Americans avoid certain subjects which are considered too personal and therefore impolite. These include questions about a person's age, financial affairs, cost of clothes or personal belongings, religion, political views, love (or sex) life, and about why you don't have children or why you are not married.

If someone happens to ask questions which seem to you to be too personal, there are ways you can avoid answering them. You can simply smile and pleasantly turn the questions aside by a comment such as "I'll tell you some other time" or "Let's talk about that when we get to know each other better," then quickly change the subject. The American will get the point but not be offended.

Terms of Address and Titles

The whole matter of titles and forms of address may be quite strange to you. Americans have little feeling for rank, especially social rank. Most do not themselves enjoy being treated with special deference for age or position; it makes them uncomfortable. Many Americans find even the terms "Mr.," "Mrs.," "Miss," or "Ms." stiff and formal. You hear people well beyond middle age say—even to quite young people—"just call me Sally (or Henry or Don)." Being on first-name terms is taken as a sign of acceptance and friendliness.

Quite often introductions are made right from the start with first names: "Mary Smith, this is John Jones." This then leaves the option open to you; you can call the woman "Mary" or you can call her more formally "Miss Smith," whichever you prefer. Sometimes both of you might use the formal address for a few minutes, then one or the other changes to first names. If you don't want to use first names so quickly, just don't. Nobody will mind.

"Ms." is a term which includes both unmarried and married women. Since men are not identified by whether they are married or not, there is no reason why women should be. "Ms." is more common in writing than in speaking. When it is spoken, it is pronounced "mizz," although many people seem to think that it is not very easy to say. Some women still accept the traditional titles of Miss and Mrs. and even prefer them, but don't be surprised if you meet women who do not.

You may notice that when Americans speak together they seldom use these titles unless they are followed by family names, as in "Mr. Johnson," "Mrs. Gray," "Ms. Wilkins." We have no equivalent to *Monsieur* or *Señor* or *Mademoiselle* or *Madame* during a conversation, as in "You're looking very well today, Mr." It would be very unusual to hear "Good morning, Mr." or "How are you, Mrs.?" If you are accustomed to hearing such forms of address interspersed throughout a conversation, their lack of use here may feel cold, impersonal, even disrespectful at first. Feel perfectly free to drop in your own "Madame," or "Señor" if you want to do so. It will sound interesting or different, even a bit flattering to the American! But do not be offended if we don't do it too.

Since class differences are minimized in this country, we do not have family titles such as Lord or Count or Duke for distinguished people. What we do use instead are occupational titles. These recognize a status that has been earned, not merely inherited. Occupations which most frequently carry titles include diplomats, members of Congress (or certain other top government posts), judges of the courts, military officers, medical doctors, professors, priests, rabbis, and Protestant clergy. Examples would be Ambassador Jones, Senator Smith, Governor Russell, Judge Harley, General Clark, Dr. Brown (medical), Dr. Green (Ph.D.), Professor Harkins, Father White, Rabbi Cohen, or Reverend Thomas.

Generally speaking, men in all other occupations are addressed as "Mr.," women as "Miss," "Mrs.," or "Ms." If in doubt as to the manner of address, never hesitate to ask. For example, you might say, "Is it *Mrs.* Smith?" "Is it *Dr.* Long?" If you are embarrassed about asking, yet want to be respectful, you can always use "Mr." or "Ms." The people you address will probably realize your dilemma and help you by telling you the proper term.

Unless you are distinguished by your occupation, you will find all formalities in address are quickly lost because a friendly, informal relationship is more important to Americans than is either rank or status. We can still respect a person even if we call him Charlie or Pedro. To us, informality does not mean lack of respect.

There are other customs in addition to a disregard for titles that visitors accustomed to considerable attention and service at home may find insulting at first. Some people may feel that insufficient deference has been paid to them in relation to their position when they are treated as everyone else is in the United States. In such cases, some cultural adjustment will contribute a great deal toward a positive experience in the United States.

A Do-It-Yourself Society

Since the United States is a do-it-yourself country, we generally carry our own bags, take our laundry to the Laundromat, stand in line at the grocery store, or shine our own shoes, whoever we may be—lawyer, professor, bank president, or corporate executive. Anyone who can afford the extremely high cost of service in this country, and wants to pay for it, may. But there is absolutely no social stigma in doing one's own daily chores, no matter how menial. In fact, Americans take pride in do-it-yourself accomplishments and may devote a great deal of their leisure time to projects around the home. As noted earlier, huge warehouse stores have been built throughout the country which cater to do-it-yourself tasks.

Many Americans who could afford household help or a driver or a gardener do not employ them. They prefer family privacy, independence, and freedom from responsibility, all of which are at least partially lost when one has help in one's home. Others would rather use their money for travel, sports, or in some other way instead of paying high American wages for domestic help. For the most part, household help has been replaced by easily operated appliances, prepared or packaged foods, wrinkle-free fabrics, and other such labor-saving developments. This doesn't mean that no one employs domestic help; many people, for example, hire a cleaning person for a few hours per week, especially if the adults in the household work full time.

People employed in this service industry and their employers are subject to the same government and business regulations as anyone else in a job. Employees share Social Security payments with their employers, for example, and jobs such as cleaning person, gardener, and chauffeur are jobs like any other to Americans, with salaries often equal to salaries of office workers or clerks or waiters.

Protocol

Those coming from countries where rank is clearly recognized feel the lack of protocol. For example, we rarely seat an honored guest in a particular position in the living room or in a car. A few formalities do exist, however; you may observe that the honored guest will normally sit to the right of the host or hostess at a dinner party and will probably be shown through a door or into an elevator first.

In Japan the back seat is the honored place in a car. If Americans have any feeling for this at all, it is likely that the front seat, next to the driver, is considered the best in a private car, partly because the driver is likely to be the host and partly because the front window offers the best view.

Blunt Speech

Don't think Americans are being rude if we tend to speak in monosyllables or answer with a mere "O.K.," "Sure," or "Nope" or greet you with "Hi." Our brevity is not a personal insult, though to those accustomed to formal phrases we seem blunt. American informality has become more desirable than formal expressions of greeting or farewell that require language based on the situation and the status of the speakers.

You may also be surprised and perhaps offended at the swearing and references to sex that you hear. These kinds of expressions have become commonplace, partly because recent music and movies are full of them and partly because all languages are constantly changing. A foreigner must develop a keen sense of observation to learn when these expressions can be used and when they are not appropriate. When you are not sure, it is best to avoid them. And if you do not understand them when someone uses them, you can quietly ask what they mean.

Americans are sometimes blunt because of embarrassment. They often find it awkward to respond gracefully if people compliment them or thank them at any length. They are likely to brush aside such courtesies because they simply do not know what to say! Thus, you hear expressions such as "Don't mention it!" or "It was nothing" or "I don't deserve it." Their intent is not to be rude; in fact they probably really like your courtesy and thoughtfulness but do not want to seem to praise themselves. One of the contradictions in American society is a high regard for modesty in some situations such as accepting compliments but a seeming immodesty regarding one's own accomplishments when applying for a job.

Silence

Many Americans find silence uncomfortable; they will fill any silence if it extends for more than a few seconds. Thus, "small talk" is an important part of most conversations. Small talk refers to topics of conversation such as the weather, movies, books, community events, or family. After saying "Hello," for example, the next comment might be, "We're having beautiful weather these days, aren't we?" Then the conversation continues with more small talk. Conversations such as this might be heard at parties, on the bus or subway, at school, in the supermarket, at sports events, and in department stores.

Instead of a period of silence, students often study with the radio playing. Homemakers may leave the television on for the "companionship" of sound, even when they are working in some other room. Drivers listen to the car radio on their way to work.

There are aspects of this American discomfort with silence that can be confusing. "Silence is golden" is a saying familiar to many foreigners who study English before they come to the United States. There really are times when Americans look for a quiet place. Some students prefer to study in silence; some parents encourage their children to be quiet; some people do not play the car radio. Thus, everyone, American and foreigner alike, must become sensitive to the desires of their neighbors and friends and even strangers to fill silence at times and to be silent at other times.

Openness

Often confusing to those newly arrived from other countries is our lack of desire for certain kinds of privacy and our strong desire for other kinds. For the most part, we are not a nation of high walls and inner courts. Our lawns often join one another without fences. Especially in small towns, friends visit each other without telephoning first and sometimes enter each other's homes without even ringing the doorbell. On the other hand, nowadays many homes have security systems which are set when people leave for the evening or go shopping or go on vacation.

The United States is a big country. We have never lived in walled cities or had to protect ourselves from warring princes in neighboring states. During our first centuries, most of the United States was so sparsely populated that neighbors were welcomed— they were not fenced out. A new face or new arrival was a cause for rejoicing. In the nineteenth century when this nation was being developed, people lived cooperatively or did not survive. They protected one another and shared their labor jointly as together they cut down forests, laid railroads, roofed barns, or husked fields of corn. They depended on each other in all phases of life.

Out of these early days has come a heritage of openness, which shows itself in many ways. You will feel it as you visit in our houses—living rooms, family rooms, dining rooms, and kitchens without doors or with half walls, no walls, or glass walls. If you come from a culture that values more privacy in work and living environments, you may have to get used to colleagues who wander into your office without knocking or people who forget to close your door when they leave the room.

The exception to this sort of openness is that when carrying on substantive business discussions or negotiations, Americans insist on privacy. The custom of conducting business amidst jangling telephones and people entering and leaving makes Americans nervous and frustrated.

Americans also value personal privacy. We need time to be alone. We live in small family groups; each person considers himself or herself a separate individual. Children are provided if possible with their own private rooms, where they like to go and close the door. In many cultures wanting to be alone is a sign that something is wrong. Not so among Americans, who will often resist the constant companionship offered by foreign friends and acquaintances. When you come to live among Americans, you will find that after an initial welcome they will tend to leave you alone unless you ask for help or seek out a closer relationship.

Social Distance and Body Contact

All human beings have a "comfort zone" regulating the distance they stand from someone when they talk. This distance varies in interesting ways among people of different cultures.

Greeks, Arabs, and South Americans, for example, normally stand quite close together when they talk, often moving their faces even closer as they warm up in a conversation. Americans find this awkward and often back away a few inches. Studies have found that we feel most comfortable about twenty-one inches apart. In much of Asia and Africa there is even more space between two people in conversation. The matter of space is nearly always unconscious, but it is interesting to observe.

The comfort zone also applies to the closeness with which people sit together, the extent to which they lean over one another in conversation, the way they move as they argue or make a strong point, or their behavior in crowded situations. Americans, for example, try to keep their bodies apart, even in a crowded elevator.

Although Americans have a relatively wide comfort zone for talking, they often communicate with their hands—not only with gestures but also with touch. They may put a hand on a person's shoulder to demonstrate warmth of feeling or an arm around a person in sympathy. They may nudge someone in the ribs to emphasize a funny story, pat an arm in reassurance, or stroke a child's head in affection. They readily take someone's arm to help him or her across a street, and they often hug one another in greeting or farewell. To many people—especially those from Asia—such body contact is unwelcome. Southern Europeans and Latin Americans, on the other hand, tend to see us as cold because we gesture and touch so little compared to them.

Americans in Motion

Americans are a restless people. Most travel whenever they get the chance. They crowd onto trains, buses and planes. In increasing numbers, they hike with packs on their backs or ride bicycles, heading for the mountains, seashore, or national parks. Highways are jammed with cars, especially on holidays. Americans are joined by millions of tourists from other countries who come to enjoy the people and the culture. Don't be surprised if you are crowded and jostled by throngs of travelers, Americans as well as those from all over the world.

3

Some Dominant American Attitudes

Challenging Authority

In much of the world, authority is not challenged, either out of respect or out of fear, and sometimes because a hierarchy of rank has been fixed for so long that people have been trained for generations never to challenge it.

In such countries children are not expected to question their teachers in school, and brilliant young scholars or inventive geniuses are hampered in technical research because they hesitate to disagree with their "superiors." Such talented people may be considered too young to have any right to present findings or offer ideas that contradict the knowledge and wisdom of their elders or change the way things are done.

The American is trained from childhood to question, analyze, search. "Go look it up for yourself," a child will be told. In many schools tasks are designed to encourage the use of a wide range of materials and individual thinking. An assignment to write a paper on the world's supply of sugar (or the gold standard, or Henry VIII, or Peruvian art) will send even a young child in search of completely unfamiliar information. From the primary grades onward, children are taught to use libraries and to search for new ideas and information. By the time they are teenagers, some young and talented scholars are making original and valuable contributions in all fields of science, from astrophysics to oceanography.

Industry is so aware of this untapped resource that each year, through national competitions, it offers awards to teenagers in order to seek out (and later employ) young people with brilliant, inquiring minds.

As seen by members of some other nations, this emphasis on questioning and searching is inappropriate. Foreigners often feel that our youth lack respect. Foreign visitors are often startled and frequently annoyed to find junior staff members daring to challenge older executives or argue points with them; they do not always like it when these young men or women make often revolutionary suggestions. An executive's own blueprints, reports, or analyses may be scrutinized in detail—perhaps even challenged—by a young person. This is not to be considered an insult or loss of face, nor is it an indication of "no confidence" in the executive's experience and ability. Our whole approach to research is different. We de-emphasize the personal. A person's *ideas* are being analyzed, not the person. To us the two are quite separate. This is the way our minds work; we are seeking facts, not challenging someone as a person. Thus, even in social conversations you will find that people often argue, pick an idea apart, ask for sources, or challenge conclusions. In general, they do not mean to be rude; they are keenly interested and merely trying to explore the *idea* in greater depth. Of course, it is true that some people do become rude and do not handle their knowledge and skills in appropriate ways. Egotistical and arrogant behavior is often repaid with alienation and contempt by colleagues in the same office. Thus, bright young men and women must learn to use their knowledge and skills in cooperative, beneficial ways.

Controlling Nature

Many people in the world—most Asians, for example—seek to discover their place in nature. Americans try instead to control nature. We speak of harnessing a river, conquering space, taming the wilderness. Asians (and many others) think more in terms of compromise, consensus, or harmony. Americans believe anything can be done if we just put our minds to it. "The difficult can be done today; the impossible takes a little longer." So the searching, challenging—sometimes arrogant—mind goes to work.

Fortunately, we are beginning to realize that we cannot control nature. We are coming to understand how we have wasted and spoiled and polluted for the sake of transient gain. We are worried now about the nation's resources, our environment, our health. You will read about this in our newspapers and hear it discussed widely wherever you go.

The Whole Truth versus Courtesy

Just as our degree of individual freedom sometimes seems excessive and therefore uncomfortable to many foreign visitors, foreign attitudes toward complete honesty seem insincere and uncertain to Americans.

In many countries people will tell you what they think you want to hear, whether or not it is true. To them, this is the polite thing to do. To Americans, it is considered misleading—even dishonest—to distort facts on purpose, however kind the motive. In the United States directness tends to have a higher priority than politeness. We are taught from childhood that "Honesty is the best policy." Elsewhere, courtesy, honor, family loyalty, or many other values might come far ahead of honesty if one were listing priorities. But with us, trust and truth are very important. Saying of a person "You cannot trust him" is one of the most serious criticisms that can be made.

In view of these value differences, it is natural that misunderstandings and irritations often occur, especially in areas where being precise is important, such as in the negotiation of contracts. A foreign businessman once said, "With us a business deal is like a courtship." Americans are not usually very good at this sort of strategy; on the other hand, you can usually count on their word. You know where you stand with them. Except in advertising and in politics, they usually will not exaggerate and promise what they do not mean in order to convince you that their product is desirable.

"How far is it to the next town?" the American asks a man standing by the edge of the road. In some countries, because the man realizes that the traveler is tired and eager to reach his destination, he will politely say, "Just down the road." He thinks this is more encouraging, gentler, and therefore the desired answer. So the American drives on through the night, getting more and more angry, feeling tricked. She thinks the man deliberately lied to her, for obviously he must have known the distance quite well.

If conditions were reversed, the American would feel she was deceiving the driver if she implied the next town was close when she knew it was really thirty-five miles farther. Although also sympathetic to the weary driver, she would say, "You have a good way to go yet; it is at least thirty-five more miles." The driver might be disappointed but would know what to expect.

This often repeated question of accuracy versus courtesy leads to many misunderstandings between people of different cultures. If you are aware of the situation in advance, it is sometimes easier to recognize the problem.

Personal Progress and Changing Jobs

In many parts of the world, personal influence is almost essential in getting ahead. One needs a "godfather," or a sponsor. Here, that is not usually true. Naturally, all people use influence sometimes, but one rarely advances far on that basis alone in the United States. Here, traits which lead to success are generally considered to be willingness to work hard (at any kind of job), scholarship or skill, initiative, and an agreeable personality. In other words, even in the area of personal progress, this is a do-it-yourself society. By and large, success is neither inherited nor bestowed. This means, therefore, that our employment practices are different from those in many other countries.

In some nations it is considered disloyal to quit a job; deep reciprocal loyalties exist between employee and employer; lifelong job security and family honor are frequently involved. This is not true in the United States. Americans consider "job-hopping" a characteristic of our mobility. We consider it a right to be able to better ourselves, to move upward, to jump from company to company if we can keep qualifying for better jobs.

This constant changing of personnel seems unreasonable to many citizens of foreign nations: "Where are your roots?" "How can you be so cold and inhuman?" "You act as if you are dealing with machines, not humans." They do not understand that a great many Americans *like* to move about. New jobs present new challenges, opportunities, friends, and experiences and often a new part of the country.

The employer may be quite content, too. Perhaps he or she has had the best of that employee's thinking; a new person may bring in fresh ideas, improved skills, or new abilities. Then, too, a newcomer, lacking seniority, will probably start at a lower salary. Changing jobs is so readily accepted here, in fact, that good employees may bounce back and forth among two or three corporations, being welcomed back to their original company more than once through their career, each time at a higher level.

Wealth and Privilege

Status symbols such as cars, color television sets, and swimming pools often confuse visitors to the States. Some cultures are accustomed to a system in which a luxury market supplies a small number of expensive goods for the rich; everyone else does without. In the United States this is not true. Because our economy operates on the basis of a mass market, blue-collar workers, miners, farmers, even people on welfare own goods that represent great wealth in some other countries. In terms of hours of work required to buy such luxuries, the cost is low. Secretaries, high school students, bank tellers, clerks, or janitors can and do buy cars, take trips abroad, and own all kinds of luxuries. Often they purchase luxuries on the installment plan, and the costs over a reasonable period of time are not prohibitive in terms of their wages. In fact, many items considered a luxury abroad are assumed a necessity here.

This difference can be perplexing for the visitor who, understandably, interprets wealth in his or her terms, thinking a Cadillac or membership in a golf club must indicate upper class and education. As a result, the visitor expects to find that the owner possesses the status that accompanies leisure in the visitor's country. This is not necessarily so. The big spender is not necessarily either educated or cultured.

Class

Americans like to claim that we are a classless society. Maximum wages, a high standard of living, mass-produced clothing, purposely casual speech, and the wide use of first names all combine to give the nation a classless appearance, especially to newcomers. But under this superficial appearance of equality, Americans are, in fact, quite conscious of class differences.

It is important to remember, however, that in the United States people can, and do, move from one class to another on their own merits (or misfortunes). To move up to a higher status, a person needs enough energy, determination, and ability to be successful at something. He or she can start as a salesperson, factory worker, taxi driver, or bank teller. Americans respect—and many are themselves proof of—the "self-made individual." You can hear these kinds of success stories all around you if you ask people about their youth: the woman whose father was a miner, and she is now a leading journalist, the man who put himself through school by selling brushes and is now president of the brush company. These are the dramatic success stories, but for every one who gets right to the top there are thousands of others who, less dramatically but nonetheless truly, climb up many steps beyond their parents on the social and economic ladder—and, of course, there are those who move down.

This constant flow of people from one social level to another indicates that both the word and the idea of "class" mean something quite different in the United States from most other countries. Not only is this nation made up of highly diverse ethnic, racial, and social strands, but its inhabitants are also enormously mobile geographically. People move from one location to another with remarkable frequency as they search for ever better positions. One statistical study reports that one out of five families moves every three years.

This ceaseless mixing and merging into new communities, this repeated adjustment to new environments and people are important factors in trying to understand the baffling question of class in the United States. The do-it-yourself, independent, questioning American personality is another factor.

In many nations a person's social position is still a group matter, shared with the family, the wider group of relatives or clan, perhaps even the whole village or district. Not so the American's. In the United States, position in society is, to a large degree, personal rather than influenced by family or group.

Before World War II, the family unit in the United States was stronger than it is now. Uncles, aunts, grandparents, and children of all ages vacationed with one another, came together for holiday festivities, and were closely knit. But as technology takes hold in any nation, social patterns are bound to change. The talented mathematician, scientist, or manager is suddenly in great demand and often moves quickly to higher levels of status and wealth. Expanding companies transfer their employees to new locations, removing them from stable family ties; more and more people settle in small houses or apartments in urban areas where grandparents and other family members can no longer share space.

The same shift is beginning to take place in other countries. Nowadays a man who can read and understand the newspaper or fix a tractor may, and often does, take over from the traditional leader. Technology puts a premium on youth, who better understand electronics, computers, nuclear energy, and the space age. Skilled young people move ahead, starting their families in new ways and locations, often giving up traditional values and customs. The "onward and upward" restlessness becomes more and more widespread and class structures are torn apart by the force of twentieth-century demands.

Frequently, it is just one member of an American family who surges ahead, becoming president of a university, head of a firm, or a well-known member of government while the rest of the family remain in modest jobs in a modest environment. When this happens, many Americans may feel no sense of commitment either to their relatives or to their community as new frontiers beckon. They may come back now and then to their former environment, but many move away, never to return. Others, of course, maintain strong ties of affection and loyalty.

Most nations derive considerable security from stable, lasting family and friendship ties. Each person is embedded in a life-long and supportive network of family and community relationships. However, the seemingly self-sufficient American is often rootless and throughout life continues to form new alliances, lose them, then move on to others.

For most people class is a competitive and changing thing. Class boundaries, therefore, overlap considerably. Studies show that four out of five Americans, when asked, describe themselves as middle class. In most other countries higher percentages of people tend to define class more precisely and therefore describe themselves either as upper class, lower class, or upper-middle or lower-middle class. Nowadays, American social and class structure is undergoing profound change. As the United States moves from an industrially based society to one based on electronics and information, the traditional blue-collar middle class is disappearing. Some worry that as the trend toward downsizing and computerization continues, the middle class will actually shrink as many displaced workers are forced into low-paying service jobs.

Success can be defined as that which gives a man or woman more status than he or she possessed before. It can be won through skill, intelligence, leadership, and sometimes sheer perseverance— regardless of birth. In the American scene success has normally been accompanied by increased financial rewards. Upward-moving people, therefore, have found themselves associated with first one and then another success level, with its accompanying financial status.

As a result, class in the United States is determined both by a person's job and by his or her pattern of consumption. Since class is a flexible, competitive state, people try to make their position clear by visible and recognizable symbols such as cars, houses, clubs, vacations, and so on. Those who have remained on the same rung of the social and economic ladder are often subtly rejected by those who have risen. Racial and ethnic discrimination should be seen in this country against the background of a much broader but less discussed tendency of many Americans to exclude one another—of any ethnic group—through fear of losing their own place. Prejudice here is in fact often as much economic as racial, though racial prejudice is a constant source of conflict which thoughtful people continually try to eliminate from our society.

Our youth are in the process of trying to work out new goals and values. A whole generation was deeply disillusioned by the Vietnam War, Watergate, and repeated exposure to corruption and wrongdoing in high places—in government, in business, and in sports, for example. Many young people still find their idealism threatened with revelations like the Iran/Contra affair, the savings and loan scandal, and the fall of sports heroes. Via television, they see and hear about corruption and extortion in the world around them, injustice in the courts, and crime in daily life—not just in the United States but worldwide. Some become cynical early. Others are complacent. They are affluent and comfortable; life for them is easy. Why worry about other people's problems?

The majority—as is always the case—fall between the two extremes. They work hard and feel a strong sense of purpose; they start earning money early to help put themselves through college; they care about the environment; they use computers or work on advanced scientific experiments; they run; they compete in tennis or baseball; they travel around the world to learn about its people with only a backpack for luggage.

The attitudes of youth and the many new social trends are complex and difficult even for Americans to interpret. No one will expect foreign visitors to do so. However, if you can understand that in the United States social position is not a stable, inherited factor, you will comprehend much about this nation.

Whenever any society is mobile and competitive, tensions are inevitable. You will be acutely aware of social tensions in American life. Could it be, however, that stress and strain are needed—anywhere—for full national vitality? Americans consider peaceful, intelligent confrontation a healthy way to examine issues and to solve problems. Unfortunately, there is sometimes destructive confrontation in our society, which hinders progress and blinds people to equitable solutions.

Ethnic Differences

A once-cherished American myth was that this nation was a great melting pot. In fact, it is not a melting pot at all. This is one of the reasons underlying the fast-shifting social patterns of today. The early settlers in this country were mostly white Anglo-Saxons, and most of these were Protestants, now often referred to as WASPs (white Anglo-Saxon Protestants). As one discovers by reading American history books, the contributions made by any incoming groups—African American, Latino, Italian, Japanese, Chinese, Irish—have never been fully recognized. At first, members of these groups worked hard to become assimilated where possible—that is, to become a part of mainstream culture. But for a large proportion of these groups assimilation has not been possible. Now, for many, it is not even considered desirable. As the years have passed, the proportion of white Anglo-Saxon Protestants to other culture groups is declining, and in places (especially big cities) WASPs have become a minority. According to the *Statistical Abstract of the United States*, 1993, published by the U.S. Department of Commerce, by the year 2000 whites will constitute only 71 percent of the U.S. population, and by 2010, only 66 percent. Clearly the social issues, both positive and negative, involved in such a shift of ethnic groups present a major challenge to the United States in the coming years.

The growing minorities, having been rejected over the years, are understandably turning back to their own ethnic and racial backgrounds, seeking their own pride and identity out of their own past histories. The most noticeable of these groups are the African Americans, Latinos, and Asians.

The whole problem of ethnic conflict in American society has been so played up in the world's media that visitors to our shores are often surprised when they see blacks and whites working side by side in offices, factories, schools, and institutions in cities across the country, and when they notice that close friendships exist across ethnic lines.

Many people of color arrive here fearing varying degrees of discrimination. Slights, insults, and narrow-mindedness do still exist, unfortunately, especially in the crucial areas of housing, schools, and jobs. There are still frictions and sometimes riots, and educational equality remains a dream. There are also many areas of the country where people of other ethnic backgrounds do not enjoy the full range of opportunities available to whites.

Real friendships between the races, full trust, and easy social encounters are still far too rare. However, even in this, the slowest area of progress, barriers are breaking down, especially among the young.

African Americans

Because the world press has concentrated mostly on the negative, with little reference to any kind of progress, newcomers may at first be surprised at the economic range they will find among African Americans. Colleges are opening the way to better jobs. Black executives, judges, elected officials, and professors are no longer rare. More and more African Americans are buying houses and apartments in middle- and upper-class neighborhoods. As everyone knows, this integration varies by locality, and progress is slow, but in the past forty years there has been much forward motion. Black visitors from abroad will experience varying degrees of acceptance, depending considerably on their own educational background, economic status, and personality. They need not fear violence or personal attack because of their race. Unfortunately, however, people are too often attacked for other reasons in our cities these days. In our large cities, ghettos are still too numerous; violent gangs, crime, and illegal drug problems are rampant in some of these areas. But some progress is being made, and black visitors will encounter much goodwill, acceptance, and friendship among both African Americans and whites.

Latino Americans

A fast-growing minority in the United States, Latino Americans consist primarily of people of Mexican heritage, living mostly in the West, Southwest, and Midwest; Puerto Ricans, concentrated largely along the east coast, especially in New York but moving in greater numbers into the Midwest; and Cuban-Americans, many of whom have settled in Florida. Latinos add a special blend of Spanish, Indian, and African cultures to the national fabric, bringing with them the heritage of the Caribbean and various parts of Central and South America. A Mexican writes of the Latino heritage in the United States:

> We explored and charted areas and regions which, for example, later became Florida, Georgia, Louisiana and Missouri. We were the first cowboys. Through our ancient knowledge of irrigation we made an oasis out of desert areas in Arizona and California. We built many of the waterways, railroads, and charted many of the original trails that became the highways of the southwest.

> —Gilbert G. Pompa, Director of Community
> Relations Service, Pontiac, Michigan,
> taken from a speech

The numbers of Latino Americans are now so great that you will find bilingual (Spanish-English) signs and instructions and bilingual schools in some parts of the country. Bilingualism, especially in the schools, is an issue of some significance in the United States and supported by many people. Others feel that efforts to provide public school instruction in a student's first language (not only Spanish but other languages as well) subvert the melting pot concept of American society and sow the seeds of disunity. Thus, you will probably encounter the "English only" debate, especially in the newspapers, where national policy on the subject is discussed.

Latino Americans are considered by many to be "sleeping giants" on the political scene. Although their political influence is not yet commensurate with their numbers, they are beginning to realize that they have the potential for power in the political arena because of their numbers (the Bureau of the Census predicts over 32 million by the year 2000). They are starting to organize politically. MAPA (the Mexican American Political Association) predicts that the five southwestern states will soon elect Latino Americans to the highest state offices—including governors and state senators—in increasing numbers. California has more citizens of Latino origin than any other state. Texas, Florida, Arizona, New Mexico, and New York also have high percentages. By the year 2000, Latino Americans will represent almost 12 percent of the population of the United States, and by 2010, almost 14 percent, according to the Department of Commerce.

Asian Americans

By the year 2000 nearly 5 percent of the population will be of Asian origin, concentrated most heavily in California, but also scattered increasingly throughout the country. Most live in cities, where they tend to cluster in Asian neighborhoods.

Roughly 7,000 Asian Americans are Indochinese refugees, called by some "a caste of survivors" because of the ordeals they experienced in leaving their countries. For the most part they have great family cohesiveness and a deep respect for education. A smaller proportion of Asians are from the subcontinent (Indians, Pakistanis, and Sri Lankans) or the Philippines.

A far larger number are of Chinese, Japanese, and Korean origins; for this group the Confucian ethic is still a strong factor in their behavior. "In that ethic," says sociologist William Liu in an article by Fox Butterfield in the *New York Times* (3 Aug. 1986), "there is a centripetal family orientation that makes people work for the honor of the family—not for themselves. The Confucian ethic is very compelling—as was the Protestant ethic in the days of America's founding fathers—a great motivator."

Asian Americans tend to have a single-minded concentration on getting ahead. They are doing notably well academically and are surging into the top universities from coast to coast—Harvard, MIT (Massachusetts Institute of Technology), University of California at Berkeley, UCLA (University of California at Los Angeles), and many others.

A tremendous "brain drain" to the United States has taken place. Asian engineers, doctors, and scientists have been coming to the States in great numbers ever since the outbreak of the Korean War (1950). Among the best known have been I. M. Pei, the architect, and An Wang and Samuel Ting, Nobel laureates in physics. The United States has also been greatly enriched by many other Asians who are successfully competing in a variety of fields.

Majority-Minority Politics

The fact that a minority will peacefully accept the outcome of a hotly contested election and the idea of cooperation among bitter political adversaries are difficult concepts for many visitors to understand. Some people fear what they call the tyranny of the majority. "How does a minority ever get heard?" they ask.

Interested visitors may want to attend a town meeting in a small American town. Here anyone may listen as citizens argue hotly, fiercely, and loudly for a long time over some local issue. Finally, the vote is called and counted. The visitor may see speakers who were bitterly opposed shake hands and offer each other a ride home. The loser does not usually feel dejected. He or she will begin immediately lining up new support (often called lobbying) or will work on the same issue through some other channel. The loss is taken in good grace: "I have to work harder to build a bigger majority" is the way the loser is likely to react.

Americans start early to learn the system. Sometimes, even from first grade onward in school, they campaign, vote, and elect class committees and class officers from among their own number. Or the teacher will appoint children to the "Fruit Juice Committee," "Goldfish Feeding Committee," "Blackboard Cleaning Committee," or similar rather ridiculous-sounding committees, found even as early as in kindergarten classes. The process of voting, the notion of responsibility, and the idea of "majority-minority" soon become familiar to young Americans. They learn to accept defeat and work toward another day—to live, in other words, within our type of governmental structure.

The American Political System

Those who come from nations where the state is supreme find personal involvement in politics baffling. "Grassroots democracy" seems to them chaotic; the relationship among our cities and towns, counties, states, and the nation is hard for them to understand.

To an American the word "state" means one of fifty geographic and fairly autonomous entities, united rather loosely by our federal government. But to an Iraqi, a Syrian, a North Korean, a Paraguayan, or to many others, a state means a strongly centralized national government with absolute powers far beyond those held by our federal authorities. To those accustomed to this sort of rule, centralized governmental power is normal and feels comfortable. Such people expect a leader to act decisively, quickly, and alone. They may have a hard time understanding the American preference for compromise, committee decision, or consultation with many people, some of whom may, in fact, be the leader's enemies. Long delays or legal quibbling while our government "tests the winds of public opinion" are often mistakenly interpreted as meaning that our president does not really care about the question or is, in fact, not sincere in his stand.

Visitors often ask, "How can there still be segregation in American schools when over forty years ago the nation's Supreme Court ruled that it was unconstitutional? Why is there a problem with crime? Why does the Congress seem unable to accomplish much?"

Because of its enormous size and the great variety of its people, the United States has developed a system that allows for doing things gradually. In constructing a large building, one allows spaces for the stretching and shrinking of metals. We operate on that same principle. Ideas proceed at different speeds in different areas and at different levels of society; an issue packed with emotion in some areas takes longer to be resolved there than elsewhere. Time must be allowed, opinions must be tested in order to preserve the diversity of this enormous country while at the same time giving it a basic framework of unity. It is cumbersome and often slow, but precisely because there is flexibility, the country has remained a unit despite its share of critical differences through the years. If these differences had been met head-on by absolute governmental decree, the nation would almost surely have split apart long ago. Many countries face such possible division within their own borders today because leeway, gradual progress toward decisions, public opinion, and other safeguards have not been built into their systems.

Since public opinion is so vitally important in the United States, our leaders must work within its boundaries. To do so, they must keep consulting, compromising, conferring, and "feeling the pulse" of the nation. Those who are accustomed to public institutions being the instruments of a central government naturally look for a unified government policy somewhere in the United States; they do not find it. They assume a country *reflects* government policy. In fact, in the United States it is more usual for public opinion to *direct* government policy. The American people, for example, demanded withdrawal from Vietnam long before the government took that stand. Black and white citizens marched and struggled and demonstrated together for civil rights so long and with such commitment that Congress finally passed the Civil Rights Act in the 1960s; it was not initiated by the government but by the people themselves. Women are demanding equality in the workplace; gays and lesbians are struggling for antidiscrimination laws based on sexual orientation. These movements gain ground because of the people, not because of any initiative by government.

What newcomers need to understand is that Americans recognize differences and allow leeway within (1) the law, (2) policy, and (3) the actual situation. These three factors often pull and tug just as a ship creaks and strains when its hull meets conflicting winds and waters. But it remains a ship, and it continues to move ahead, however slowly. It does this because it has play in its joints. Therefore, like the ship, the country does not sink but can stay afloat even under heavy stress.

Let us look at the deeply divisive national problem of civil rights:

1. *The law:* By federal law there is now neither legal nor constitutional discrimination against anyone because of race.

2. *Policy:* The federal policy is that discrimination is illegal and should be phased out "with all possible speed."

3. *The facts:* All too slowly, with uneven pace, sometimes two steps forward and one step back, faster in some states than in others, the United States is making attempts to end discrimination.

The country has been struggling for a long time with countless other serious issues that occur at national, state, local, and personal levels, gradually working out accommodations and resolving various kinds of problems. Despite deep regional, emotional, and personal differences, the nation will be kept on course throughout this process by the law of the land.

It is often difficult for those from highly centralized nations to understand, but the fact is that final power really *does* lie in the hands of the people in the United States. This is true whether one speaks of political, economic, or social power. Americans distrust and will not long tolerate being pushed by an authoritarian leader or government. They want to keep power decentralized; they like it that way. Social issues such as civil rights, illegal immigration, divorce laws, equality of pay for women, abortion laws, gay and lesbian rights, and health care are therefore hotly debated for a long time at both the state and national levels. National law reflects many state differences and attitudes. Change comes slowly, after endless debate. But those changes which finally become the law of the land mostly do so eventually with the consent of a nationwide majority. Thus, most laws remain stable once in place.

The American Way of Giving

Americans are highly motivated to contribute financially to causes in which they believe. Thus they give generously to colleges and universities; hospitals and other nonprofit institutions; charitable, religious, and relief organizations; and environmental groups.

The American system of private philanthropy parallels our system of private enterprise. Huge trusts and family foundations provide millions of dollars annually for charitable causes. Besides those large donors, however, there are millions of individuals who make direct contributions to charities. Thus, schools, businesses, factories—almost any place where there are employees—encourage people to contribute. One of the best-known methods is through the United Way, an umbrella organization which collects contributions and then distributes them in the form of money, clothing, or food to various worthy causes. Offices have "drives" of a week to a month during which the employees try to raise a certain amount of money, their goal for that particular year.

In addition, many organizations raise money through direct mail appeals. Letters from those organizations arrive in the mail often, and individuals choose which ones, if any, they will send contributions to. No one is obligated to contribute, but many people do, to whatever extent they are able.

Throughout the year, but especially at Thanksgiving and Christmas, charitable organizations collect new or used clothing, toys, and food to distribute to the poor and needy. In addition, "walkathons" and "telethons" are held during which people contribute to charitable organizations and causes through pledges they make of certain amounts of money. For example, each year many cities hold AIDS walks, during which participants walk a mile or several miles in order to raise funds for AIDS victims and AIDS research. Friends of those who walk pledge an amount of money based on the distance walked. During telethons, which sometimes last for twenty-four hours, people pledge contributions by calling the television station while the telethon is being broadcast.

Besides wanting to help those in need, Americans are provided with tax incentives in the form of tax deductions for charitable contributions. When individuals file their tax returns each year, they are allowed deductions for various kinds of charitable contributions. This is the way the American system helps charitable organizations to continue their good work.

4

Doing Business in the United States

U.S. Government Policy

The general policy of the U.S. government has been to admit and treat foreign capital on an equal basis with domestic capital. Except in a few sensitive areas (such as communications, defense, and coastal shipping), there are few federally imposed limitations on foreign investment in the United States. However, under their own constitutions, some states have considerable power in regulating investment that falls under their jurisdiction. State laws need to be carefully understood in any business matters. Every state also has its own tax system, regulating all localities within its borders. From state to state, matters such as the availability of skilled labor, requirements for pollution control, and the like vary widely.

In 1974 the federal Committee on Foreign Investment in the United States was established to monitor the impact of direct foreign investment in the country. At present, the U.S. branches or subsidiaries (above a certain size) of foreign parent companies must register by filing quarterly reports with the U.S. Department of Commerce.

New arrivals doing business in the United States will find that U.S. economic strength has traditionally been built on the private business sector. Monopolies, cartels, and other restraints of trade are prevented by law. Some industries—for example, banking, insurance, transportation, and utilities—are government-regulated in varying degrees, but, although there are many complaints about government paperwork, there is, in fact, far less federal regulation than in many other highly developed economies.

Much of the required paperwork results from close scrutiny by a wide range of government agencies over such matters as taxation, consumer protection, food and drugs, environmental controls, and equal labor opportunities. Many such protections have, in fact, been added as a result of the efforts of concerned citizens.

Labor Unions

A new arrival will find considerable differences regarding trade unions, largely because of the enormous size of the country and the diversity of American workers. There are several national unions but most of these operate through regional or local chapters. The extent to which labor is organized at all varies a good deal, depending on both the type of industry and the region of the country. The amount of power a given union can exert also varies considerably. The most highly unionized industries are mining, construction (including all its subdivisions such as electrical work and plumbing), manufacturing, printing, airlines, and public utilities. Among the least unionized are the professions such as medicine and law, banking and insurance.

Contracts between management and unions are for fixed periods of time, enforceable by law. "Wildcat," or unauthorized, strikes are rare; authorized strikes usually take place as a contract expires, almost as part of the bargaining process. Very often both labor and management know about them in advance and plan accordingly.

Labor unions have been under considerable pressure from well-organized and well-financed business organizations determined to reduce union power. In earlier years organized labor had great political power, working to elect those candidates across the country who would represent their interests in the legislative process. But business has begun employing its own election strategies and developing strong political action committees that are now working hard to support business-oriented candidates at every level of government—national, state, and local.

Women in the Working World

During the second quarter of 1979 American women passed a milestone. More than 50 percent of those over sixteen years of age were reported to be in the labor force, full- or part-time. In 1991 that number increased to almost 58 percent. Their influx into the job market continues at a rapid pace. Most are still employed in jobs traditionally filled by women: clerical, sales, production, education, and service. Growing numbers, however, are moving into the higher-level, well-paid positions and professions once reserved almost exclusively for men. Analysts expect this trend toward increased numbers of women in the workforce to continue, in no small measure because inflation and rising costs make it necessary for women to work, and also because more and more women choose to work at careers outside the home. In many families two paychecks are now required to meet the high costs of a moderate standard of living. The poor have always struggled to make ends meet; now the middle class are also struggling.

With the decline in the birthrate, the high divorce and separation rate, and the subsequent rush of women into the workplace, it is hard to find the once-typical family consisting of father at work, mother in her apron at home, and two children. This profile accounts for less than 7 percent of all American families, difficult though that may be to believe. Today it is far more common for families to be headed by a single parent or for both parents to be working, managing their lives in ways unpredictable even twenty years ago.

"For us it works out well," said one father who splits house and child care with his wife, an airline flight attendant. "I know the children much better than I did, the quality of time we all spend together is better, the children have adjusted easily, and working has added an important new dimension to my wife's life."

Not all families are so liberated. The day-to-day management of families can, in fact, be quite difficult for working women who still do most of the household tasks as well, fitting them into weekends and evenings after a full day at work.

Society is groping for ways to adjust to the rush of women into the workforce. Much research is being done on the impact of this trend on the stability of families. Interestingly, to date it has been shown that there is little relationship between employed women and divorce. In fact busy wives and higher double incomes seem to be a factor toward greater stability. Social observers who formerly predicted the decline of family life in the United States are now revising their predictions. They say there are signs that the divorce rate is no longer climbing. More people are getting married later—with greater maturity. It is teenage marriages which still are the most likely to end in divorce. Unmarried "cohabitation"—or shared living—is common now at all social levels, especially if there are no children.

There is growing recognition that the family is a diverse and complex entity, the traditional family being only one of its forms. In these days of steadily rising costs and increasing financial pressure, the family is not likely ever to revert to its old traditional form.

Job Sharing and Part-Time Work

A relatively new trend resulting from changing values and lifestyles is the increase in part-time or job-shared work. Growing numbers of people, both men and women, are reducing their income and job responsibilities in order to gain time for other pursuits—sharing child-care responsibilities or developing fuller lives for themselves. They may want to learn new skills, study, conduct research, take part in sports, or simply live with less pressure. Also, many who are old enough to retire prefer to keep active by working a few hours a day or a few days a week.

Most businesses are receptive to this change and, indeed, encourage it because in many cases it enables them to avoid paying benefits such as pension plans and health insurance they must provide full-time employees.

Rather than a deterioration of the work ethic, this interest in part-time work reflects a reordering of priorities. Adjustments can be made to accommodate education, work, family responsibilities, and leisure, though at varying levels of intensity. Furthermore, communities may benefit from the additional time that is devoted to worthwhile activities such as volunteering at a hospital or making improvements on one's home, and from the increase in the number of available jobs.

There is sense to the trend; all may benefit when the system accommodates people who need to work but do not need (or want) to do so full-time.

Attitudes toward Foreign Investments in the United States

Americans are worried about reports of increasing numbers of foreigners gaining control of assets, including property, worth millions of dollars in the United States. "When we turn ownership of our heritage—our property and our resources—over to outside people, we are giving them political power. That is the same thing as economic power; we should recognize it as such," said one concerned businessman. Workers across the country worry about working under foreign bosses. Few realize that the amount of U.S. money invested abroad in other people's countries is still about four times that of foreign money invested in the United States. Still fewer have any understanding of the extent to which foreign money is then being reinvested again in the United States, nor do they understand the benefits derived from that investment.

In short, you will find Americans echoing exactly the same objections often voiced by people in other countries when foreign firms invest heavily in their economies. However, most Americans have foreign roots and many still feel the pull of old ties. As individuals, most people from abroad can expect to be welcomed, even though the notion of "foreigners" in the abstract may raise suspicion. The problem of illegal immigration has made

Americans aware of those who are here with proper visas and those who are not. With resources and jobs steadily decreasing, some states, especially those that border Mexico, have made illegal immigration a political issue. The question is, should states pay for social services such as education and health care for those who are here illegally?

On the other hand, the many Americans who are profiting from foreign investment naturally welcome the trend and, therefore, will also welcome sojourners to this country. Foreign-owned plants are warmly received when they are established in areas where additional jobs, investments, and tax revenues are needed. Real estate dealers are, of course, delighted. Many large-scale farmers have sold land at great profit to foreign buyers. Many states—and even many cities—are actively competing abroad for foreign investment, offering special tax exemptions and favorable financing to investors who settle in their areas. Those who come bringing business with them are likely to perceive no mood of isolationism.

5

Business Attitudes and Practices

Because people operate out of their heritage—influenced by their own historical and cultural pasts—there is necessarily a wide range of differing values, priorities, and behaviors that affect the way life is lived and business conducted around the world.

Risk Takers and Experimenters

North Americans come from a frontier past. Many of them stem from rebel stock. They are descendants of people who braved terrible hardships in order to flee conditions at home and who took great risks to settle a new land. That same spirit has motivated wave after wave of immigrants to come to the United States, leaving one world and seeking another. Indochinese, Haitians, Cubans, and Koreans are among the most recent groups to arrive on these shores. The nation's frontier past and the subsequent waves of determined immigrants have forged a strong element of risk taking in the nation's character. We are always looking for the next frontier, a new challenge.

This exploratory element, coupled with what once seemed like limitless raw materials, has also made us careless with materials. We scrap a machine, a product, or a process in favor of something new if we consider the new to be better, faster, stronger, safer. To people from countries where raw materials have always been scarce and where conserving has necessarily been a high priority, this is often shocking. The philosophy that it is "cheaper to scrap the old and replace it with something better" frequently seems to them to be both wasteful and foolhardy.

The American view is that no one stands still. If you are not moving ahead, you are falling behind. This attitude results in a nation of people geared, to a large degree, to researching, experimenting, and exploring. Most of its adventurer, rebel, or refugee stock has come here only during the last two hundred years. The country is young and full of vitality.

Time

There are two elements that Americans save carefully: time and labor.

"We are slaves to nothing but the clock," it has been said. Time is treated as if it were an almost tangible entity. We *budget* it, *save* it, *waste* it, *steal* it, *kill* it, *cut* it, and *account* for it; we also *charge* for it. Time is a precious commodity. Many people have a rather acute sense of the shortness of each lifetime. Once the sands have run out of a person's hourglass, he or she cannot be replaced. We want every minute to count.

Since people value time highly, they resent someone else "wasting" it beyond a certain courtesy point. This view of time may be one of the causes of our lack of patience. In the American system of values, patience is not a high priority. We begin to move restlessly about if we feel time is slipping away without some return—either in terms of pleasure, work accomplishment, or rest. Those coming from lands where time is looked upon differently may find this matter of pace to be one of their most difficult adjustments in both business and daily life.

Many newcomers to the States will miss the opening courtesies of a business call. For example, they will miss the ritual socializing that goes with a welcoming cup of tea or coffee that may be traditional in their own country. They may miss leisurely business chats in a cafe or coffeehouse. Normally, Americans do not assess their visitors in such relaxed surroundings over prolonged small talk; nor do they take them out for dinner or a round on the golf course while they develop a sense of trust and rapport. Rapport to most of us is less important than performance. We seek out credentials of past performance rather than evaluate a business colleague through social courtesies. Since we generally assess and probe professionally rather than socially, we start talking business very quickly.

Most Americans live according to time segments laid out in engagement calendars. These calendars may be divided into intervals as short as fifteen minutes. We often give a person two or three (or more) segments of our calendar, but in the business world we almost always have other appointments following whatever we are doing. Time is therefore always ticking in our heads.

As a result, we work hard at the task of saving time. We produce a steady flow of labor-saving devices; we communicate rapidly through fax machines, phone calls, e-mail (electronic mail), and memos rather than through personal contacts, which, though pleasant, take longer. We therefore save most personal visiting for lunch, after-work hours, or for weekend social gatherings.

To us the impersonality of electronic communication has little or no relation to the importance of the matter at hand. In some countries no major business is carried on without eye contact, requiring face-to-face conversation. In the States, too, a final agreement will normally be signed in person. However, people are meeting increasingly on television screens, conducting "teleconferences" to settle problems not only in this country but also—by satellite—internationally. An increasingly high percentage of normal business is being done these days by voice or electronic device. Mail is slow and uncertain and is growing ever more expensive.

The United States is definitely a telephone, fax, and Internet country. This is due partly to the fact that telephone service is good here, whereas postal service is less efficient. Furthermore, the costs of secretarial labor, printing, and stamps are all soaring. The telephone is quick and familiar. We can do our business and get an answer in a matter of moments. Furthermore, several people can confer together without moving from their desks, even in widely scattered locations. In a big country this, too, is important.

In today's electronic culture, nothing matches the immediacy of e-mail. Businesses and individuals are substituting e-mail for envelopes and stamps, and even the fax machine. With a modem instead of a telephone or fax, computer data can be transferred from one location to another with great speed and efficiency. The word "Internet" is derived from two words, *inter*connected and *net*works. Businesses and individuals who are connected to one of these telecommunications services have access to files, mail, forums, and a great deal of data.

Some new arrivals will come from cultures where it is considered impolite to work too quickly. Unless a certain amount of time is allowed to elapse, it seems in their eyes as if the task being considered were insignificant, not worthy of substantial respect. Assignments are thus perceived to be given added weight by the passage of time. In the United States, however, it is taken as a sign of competence to rapidly solve a problem or complete a job successfully. Usually, the more important a task is, the more capital, energy, and attention will be poured into it in order to "get it moving."

Letting Emotions Show

Compared with some cultures (Asian, for example), many people in the United States make little effort to hide their emotions. This is a high-pressure country and, especially in the cities, most people live and work under a range of stresses at home and at work. Most of us understand this fact and therefore make allowances for each other fairly readily. Our feelings are not easily hurt. "Joe is pretty uptight today," we will say, or "The meeting must have gone badly," but we are not often deeply wounded by what is said in a moment of irritation. While no one likes to be the target of someone else's anger, no one loses a great deal of "face" or status if he or she shows various degrees of emotion occasionally. Pleasure and excitement are equally readily expressed. On the whole, most of us could not be described as reserved, contained, disciplined people. Take us as we are: noisy, energetic, excitable, often quick-tempered, but usually open—easy to read and understand. Many of us, particularly businesspeople, tell each other (and will tell you) exactly where we stand on any issue. You will find this has both good and bad aspects. Many may find this to be an area of real adjustment when first encountering the American business world.

Directness and Confrontation

Closely related to the need to get on with the job without delay is another widespread American characteristic—*directness* (sometimes also called bluntness—see pages 14-15). Again, commonly used expressions reveal our priorities:

> get down to brass tacks
>
> don't beat around the bush
>
> let the chips fall where they may
>
> put your cards on the table
>
> tell it like it is

It is quite normal for us to jump right into a subject and say exactly what is on our minds. We often do not disguise our comments in carefully worded phrases to save a person's face or to allow for what Latinos would call *personalismo* or the Japanese would call *tatemae*. We are not likely to withdraw from a clear-cut confrontation between two issues.

Such directness often leads to confrontation and argument. Rather than avoiding opposing viewpoints, many Americans will readily express an opinion, expecting someone else to disagree with them. You will find lively discussions of issues at parties, at sports events, in the subway, on the bus, in the classroom, at the office—in short, almost anywhere. There are some who refuse to compromise. For them, a certain viewpoint is right or wrong, black or white, good or bad; there is no middle ground. Others are more flexible, willing to listen to the opposite side and perhaps even be persuaded to change their minds.

The opposite of telling it like it is, is *indirectness*. Many of the world's people do their best to avoid confrontations. They talk around a point, leaving room for retreat or a change of view on either side, showing their sense of respect for the other person by avoiding direct denials or negatives. An American might say, "This shipment *must* go out tomorrow," and if the reply is, "It is *impossible* for it to go out tomorrow because…," there will probably be a confrontation, with both parties giving reasons for their points of view, trying to win the argument. The same conversation among those who prefer indirectness or a face-saving style might go like this:

> Manager: "I certainly hope this shipment can go out no later than tomorrow because…."

> Aide: "I think we may have a few problems. It may be a little bit difficult, but we will try our best."

Both know from that answer that the shipment is unlikely to go out tomorrow. However, the fact is not laid on the line directly; no one will lose face whether it does or does not; the rough spots are smoothed. Both will try to adjust accordingly; each understands the other clearly.

Those who come from countries which operate in this manner may find American directness hard to accept, until they get used to the pattern and realize that nothing is meant personally. Their personal feelings may be hurt from time to time as they look for grace, for kindness, or for dignity. Though far more courteous, indirection is a slow approach. Americans look for speed, for facts, for clarity of meaning. The difference is a matter of priorities. (See "The Whole Truth versus Courtesy" in chapter 3.)

Competition

The predominant goal of business in the United States is financial profit, which is often referred to as "the bottom line." It is not family honor, personal prestige, state revenues, or any of various other goals that are primary concerns in other cultures. We spend vast sums on nationwide advertising campaigns—we compete for markets from every billboard, newspaper, and television screen. Hurried working lunches at one's desk, quick flights to do business in far places are part of this competitive pattern. So is the growing number of "workaholics." These are people who want so much to get to the top or make a corporate name for themselves that they scarcely take time out for their own families, for recreation, or for pleasure.

Decision Making

Contrary to the custom in many countries, decisions are made at various working levels in most American firms. They do not all get made at the top, as is a familiar pattern in many countries. Department, division, and section heads in the United States frequently consult with those colleagues and subordinates who have relevant knowledge. Then, depending on the type and magnitude of the decision being made, they will either make a judgment themselves or take the matter to another higher level. Even top executives normally consult one or more individuals—perhaps a board of trustees, directors, or advisers—if the matter is important, before making their own final, sometimes lonely, decision.

Negotiating

In this country negotiating is carried on in an open and direct manner at the negotiating table. It is rarely a rubber-stamp confirmation of a decision already made elsewhere, in private discussions. Americans press hard. One can assume that their eyes are firmly focused on the profit potential, whether this be long-term or short-term. Like businesspeople in most countries, they bargain. Their first figure should be considered negotiable. When they lower a price, this should not be read as a sign of uncertainty or lack of trustworthiness, though it may seem so to those whose normal negotiating patterns do not involve bargaining. In the United States, compromises are the name of the negotiating game—"I will do this if you will do that."

Putting things down on paper—initial drafts—can seem threatening to people who normally do not put matters on paper until they are firm. Americans, however, find it imperative to get basic essentials down on paper so they can think them over and discuss, revise, and reevaluate them. No one should feel that a first draft is binding; it is not. *Nothing* is ultimately binding until it is signed by both parties. No one can be held legally responsible until that point, although "gentlemen's agreements" and shared expressed perceptions are normally honored as the proceedings develop.

Most foreign businesspeople who negotiate with Americans will already have had experience along these lines. If not, they should discuss American approaches and procedures with a number of people in advance. Negotiating is always a complex process. It is a sensitive area in which cultural differences, priorities, and values play a particularly significant role. This fact should be understood from the start.

Because of conflicts experienced by enterprises doing business internationally, more and more emphasis has been placed on the need for formal intercultural training. Some firms have built in this training by employing full-time trainers; others obtain the services of professional trainers as needed. The cross-cultural awareness resulting from such training has apparently made negotiations easier and increased efficiency and thus profitability.

Tax Evasion

Naturally, nobody enjoys paying taxes, wherever they live. However, where governments back massive welfare, housing, or school programs and build miles of highways, they must have money. Tax evasion in the United States is considered "fraud" and is looked upon as a serious offense. Computers check the tax returns of rich and poor alike; audits from the Internal Revenue Service are widespread. When rich tax evaders are caught, they are subject to the same penalty rates that apply to the poor. This is not true in all countries—as many readers well know. But here tax evasion is front-page scandal when a wealthy, highly placed person or a corporation is found evading the tax laws. According to American law, private interests are subordinate to public good. Since tax evasion is regarded as affecting the welfare of the entire community and nation, it is looked upon as a major offense—not worth trying!

6

Life in the Office

Some office procedures may be unfamiliar, and matters of time and pace may be different. For most offices the work day normally starts at 9:00 A.M. This means nine sharp—not ten past or half past. You will find some people taking liberties with their starting times, but employers notice this even though they do not necessarily reprimand.

Employees in many nations have a philosophy that one works when the boss is present; but any time he or she is not there, if there is nothing specific or pressing to do, one can relax by reading the newspaper, talking with other employees, or otherwise passing the time in a personal way. In the States one is being paid for one's *time*. Employees are expected to find other work if their own desks are clear, to finish anything pending from previous days, or to help others with their work—but *never* to sit idle. The employer expects value for the money being spent. The saying "time is money" means exactly that. Many employers work as hard as, if not harder than, the employees, often working through the lunch hour and even taking work home at night.

Employees' lunch hours should be kept within the allotted time (unless one is officially discussing company business). Long lunchtime absences may be overlooked now and then, but not habitually. Also, although others may start getting ready to leave the office a few minutes early, new employees should be careful not to cut the day short. Work until the day officially ends at five o'clock, unless you are in an office where flexible schedules are the accepted procedure.

Increasingly, people are working on "flextime," which means staggered hours for arriving and departing. It is designed to ease congested roads and crowded commuter trains and to fit better with individuals' personal and family requirements. In 1991 over 15 percent of the workforce (approximately 12,118,000 people) were on flextime. Interestingly, the looser time system appears to result in greater worker productivity, higher morale, and less absenteeism.

A new word is also coming into the nation's vocabulary: "telecommuter." This refers to people who do their work from home—or from a convenient office near home—and are in contact with their headquarters by computer. Whether this will become really widespread or not is yet to be seen. Many people miss the sociability and stimulus of the office and do not want to work out of their homes, but it is certainly a new option and one that is likely to spread.

Hiring and Firing

Those from cultures where families have close bonds are accustomed to family ties being closely connected with business. This rarely happens in the United States (except for small businesses being passed down to a son or daughter or one owned by several relatives)—and is generally distrusted. We call it "nepotism" and fear it as a corrupting influence or the taking of unfair advantage over outsiders. Nor do we develop a *patron* or permanent relationship between employer and employee. In many countries people relax once they have a job, knowing they will almost never be fired (except for a major violation of law or morality). Although there are legal protections in the United States so that employees cannot be unjustly fired without cause, jobs nevertheless are not permanent. Workers must do a good job, produce well, and get along with their colleagues—or they can be fired, or "let go," as it is called. This is rarely done without warning, but it is important to be aware of the fact that in the United States one is a member of a business firm and not a family. It makes a difference.

Informality

The informality found in many offices here can prove to be a difficult adjustment for those who are accustomed to clearly defined rank in offices. The protocol of rank often exists here too, especially in large city banks, law firms, or major corporations. But in many establishments the atmosphere is informal and relaxed, with considerable joking, teasing, and wandering in and out of offices among all levels of employees. This may be perplexing at first for a newcomer who does not realize that, despite the informal use of first names and lots of small talk, people really know very well who is in charge. The manager, the shop foreman, the "boss" do hold authority, though outward signs of this authority may not be clearly visible. To people from some countries there will be a real adjustment as they find themselves working under—or as coequals with—women. This happens more frequently in some areas of the country and in some businesses than others, but generally women are increasingly evident in executive and managerial jobs.

Informal clothing such as sweaters, sports jackets, and sports shoes are worn in many offices, especially those outside the large cities. In some areas even blue jeans, shorts, or open-necked shirts are common. This should not be taken for lack of respect as might be assumed in some countries. Here it has to do with local custom, or the weather, but does not relate to respect.

Social Life

Social life among employees varies tremendously from office to office. Big corporations may have singing groups, bowling or baseball teams, trips, dance classes, or other employee activities, which you can join or not as you like. Small companies usually do not.

It is quite acceptable for men or women colleagues, single or married, to go out together for lunch. This may be the extent to which you are invited to socialize with office friends. Although many Americans readily invite colleagues to come to dinner at their homes, some do not want to mix business and social life. If this is the case in your place of work, you will have to seek your friendships through other channels.

If people rush quickly out of the office in the evening without any courtesies, think nothing of it. Often they must travel long distances to get home and are hurrying to catch special trains or buses.

Staff Meetings

Staff meetings are a regular part of most office routines. Those of all ranks are expected to contribute freely to the discussion if they have something worthwhile to add or suggest. They are not expected to make long speeches or to speak too many times in the course of a meeting. Make your point briefly and clearly, then be quiet unless asked to develop it more fully. If you have something worth saying, never hesitate because you feel too inexperienced or too new. People will think you have no ideas unless you express them.

Coffee Breaks

Nearly all large offices and factories have midmorning and mid-afternoon coffee breaks. Although fifteen minutes are allotted twice a day for relaxation and conversation, many office employees take coffee to their desks and keep on working. In small offices, the coffeepot is often on all day, and employees have coffee whenever they like or they can make tea for themselves.

Collections

Don't be startled if someone asks you to make a contribution toward a wedding or retirement present for a fellow employee. This is often done. Everyone is likely to contribute a small amount so that a gift can be given in the name of the whole office. You never refuse, whether or not you know—or like—the particular recipient. The amount per person is always small, and the requests are infrequent. When you leave, you will have some recognition too!

Perquisites, or "Perks"

At the upper staff levels there are often some perquisites, such as club memberships, cars, and the like; in addition, salespeople may take customers fishing or hunting, to sports events, or to theaters to attract their business. However visible, perks play far less of a role in the United States than in many countries. Invisible perks include medical and life insurance, financial consulting, pensions, child-care facilities, and a variety of similar benefits.

Business Cards

Business cards are widely used in the United States but not as immediately or universally as they are in some countries. Do with yours whatever is comfortable but do not be surprised if host businesspeople in the United States do not produce their cards at moments which would seem normal to you. Generally, they are exchanged in this country when two people decide they want to be in touch with each other again—not usually at the moment of meeting.

Sexual Harassment

Federal and state laws in the United States have been enacted which make sexual harassment illegal, and thus it cannot be tolerated in the workplace. If you come to the United States to work or to attend school, you should ask about company and school policy related to this issue. It is important for everyone to know what it is. This policy grew out of the principle that men and women have equal status in every facet of life and thus deserve respect from each other. Since harassment can manifest itself in many forms, it is important for employers and employees to understand the law and their company's official policy.

7

Manners and Courtesies in Social Life

Friendships

In this mobile society of ours, friendships can be close, intense, generous, and real, yet fade away in a short time if circumstances change. Both may exchange Christmas greetings for a year or two, perhaps a few letters for a while—then no more. If the same two people meet again by chance, even years later, they often pick up the friendship where it left off and are delighted. This can be perplexing to those from countries where friendships develop more slowly but then become lifelong attachments, with mutual obligations, extending sometimes deeply into both families.

In the United States you can feel free to visit in people's homes, share their holidays, enjoy their children and their lives without fear that you are taking on a lasting obligation. Do not hesitate to accept hospitality even though you cannot reciprocate. No one will expect you to do so, for they know you are far from home. Americans will enjoy welcoming you and be pleased if you accept their hospitality.

Another difficulty for many people from other countries is that although Americans include them warmly in their personal everyday lives, they do not demonstrate a high degree of courtesy if it requires a great deal of time. This is the opposite of the practice in some nations, where people are unstintingly generous with their time but do not necessarily admit a guest into the privacy of their home. In some countries hosts will appear at airports in the middle of the night to meet even a casual acquaintance; they put their car at the visitor's disposal; they take days off to act as guides—all evidence of impressive generosity. But these same people may never introduce their wives or invite the guest to participate in their family life. In both cases the feeling is equally warm; the pattern of expression, however, is different.

Distances, pace, and the pressures of life are tremendous in the United States. Also, without household help, cooking and baby-sitting and other domestic responsibilities must be absorbed into each person's day (as well as all professional, community, and social demands). As a result of these pressures and demands, many Americans will extend their welcome warmly at home but truly cannot manage the time to do a great deal with a visitor outside of their daily routine. They will probably expect you to get yourself from the airport to your hotel by public transport; they assume that you will phone them from there. Unless you are chairman of the board or a similar dignitary, you may be expected to find your own way (by cab) from the hotel to the host's office (or home). However, once you arrive there, the welcome will be full and warm and real. Most visitors find themselves readily invited into many homes here. In some countries it is considered inhospitable to entertain at home, offering what is considered "merely" home-cooked food, instead of doing something special for your guest. Restaurant entertaining indicates more respect and welcome. Also, for various other reasons such as crowded space, privacy, language difficulties, or family custom, outsiders are not invited into homes.

In the United Sates both methods are used, but here it is often considered more friendly to invite a person to one's home than to go to a public place, except in purely business relationships. The farther one is from big cities, the more likely this becomes. So if your host or hostess brings you home, do not feel that you are being shown inferior treatment.

Don't feel neglected if you do not find flowers awaiting you in your hotel room either. This happens graciously in Thailand, the Philippines, the Caribbean, Holland, and many other countries where flowers are inexpensive and plentiful. Flowers here, though, are exceedingly expensive, hotel delivery is uncertain, and arrival times are often delayed, changed, or cancelled—so flowers are not customarily sent as a welcoming touch. Please do not feel unwanted! Outward signs vary in different cultures; the inward welcome is what matters, and this will be real.

Parties

Among the more interesting customs to observe as you travel the world are the ways in which people conduct themselves at parties. In some countries men and women drift to opposite ends of the room and talk to one another; in others they sit in large chairs around the edge of the room and talk only to the people on either side of them, or silently eat and observe the scene. It is normal in some countries for people to remain patiently silent until introductions have been made, then to talk only to those to whom they have been properly introduced.

When you first arrive at a large party, the host (nowadays this term refers to male or female) may introduce you to two or three people nearby, but if others are still arriving, he or she may then leave to greet newcomers, expecting you to go on by yourself, moving from group to group. If this feels too uncomfortable, it is quite all right to say to someone, "I am a stranger here and do not know anyone. Could you introduce me to some of the people?" Most people will feel flattered that you turned to them for help and will gladly escort you around the room, introducing you and easing your discomfort.

Americans move about a great deal at parties. At small gatherings they may sit down, but as soon as there are more people than chairs in a room—or better yet, a little before this point—you will see first one and then another make some excuse to get up (to fetch a drink or greet a friend or get something to eat) until soon everyone is standing, moving around, chatting with one group and then another. Sitting becomes boring beyond a certain point. We expect people to move about and be "self-starters." It is quite normal for Americans to introduce themselves; they will drift around a room, stopping to talk wherever they like, introducing themselves and their companions. If this happens, you are expected to reply by giving your name and introducing the person with you; then the men, at least, generally shake hands. Sometimes women do so as well. A man usually shakes a woman's hand only if she extends it. Otherwise, he just nods and greets her.

After such an informal introduction, you usually talk together for a little while. Here are some of the inevitable questions you'll be asked, probably by several people: "Are you new here?" "How long have you been in America?" "Did you bring your family with you?" "What do you do?" (meaning what sort of work do you do?). Within a moment or two, you will hopefully have found something to talk about and the conversation will move along for a while. Then either person can feel free to say something informal like, "Well, it's been nice to meet you" or "I hope to see you again soon." This is the signal for both people to move to another group.

The basic rule at big parties is this: Don't stay in one place too long. Pick out people you think look interesting, then go talk to them. Women should not cluster in a group with each other. They, too, move around the room, either with their husbands, their escorts, or alone, whichever they prefer. The point of a party in this country is to meet and talk with people; the fact that you are all there together under your host's roof is in itself a form of introduction, in our view. As a result, anyone can feel free to talk to anyone else.

Our easy-come-and-go pattern is unfamiliar to people from many other countries. Like much else about the nation, it stems in large measure from our size, our numbers, and our constantly shifting population.

Invitations

Written
One should answer any written invitation as soon as possible. Some will have R.S.V.P. or "Please reply" written at the bottom. Such invitations require an answer, but even if such a request is

not included, it is still a courtesy to let the host know whether or not you expect to attend. If a telephone number is given, you can phone; otherwise, it is best to write a short note, either accepting or expressing your regrets.

By Telephone

In the United States most invitations will be in person or by an informal telephone call. When accepting an invitation, always make it a habit to repeat four things: (1) the day of the week, (2) the date, (3) the time, and (4) the place. You may say, for example, "Let me make sure I have the details straight: Tuesday, January 11, 7:30, at your home." Then you are sure you have understood it correctly.

If you do not know how to get to the host's home, this is the moment to ask for directions and to write them down. A good way to make sure you have the directions correct is to repeat each phrase as the host says it (for example, "Turn right on Broadway"), and when the directions are completed, repeat all of them once more.

Since telephones are so widespread that communication is easy in the United States, it is considered thoughtless and rude to accept an invitation and then not appear without phoning your regrets *in advance*. If something prevents you from attending, you should always telephone your host immediately, just as soon as you know you will not be able to go. Briefly explain the circumstances and express your apologies. The host may want to invite someone else in your place or, if you are the guest of honor, may change the date of the party to suit your schedule.

Announcements

Much social life in this country takes place at communal parties of one kind or another—group activities sponsored by a church, a school, a company division, or a club. These may be dinners, picnics, tours, weekend camping or skiing trips, lectures, concerts, receptions, bowling evenings, or any of a wide variety of affairs. If you have some connection with the sponsoring group, you can assume that you will be welcome to join in any such gathering. Many others are open to you whether or not you have a connection. If you see a poster announcing an event, or read a notice, or find a note in the newspaper, don't wait to be invited. Just go if you wish; no one else will receive a personal invitation either. The announcement may read "Open to the Public." Such community affairs are friendly and an excellent way to meet new people. If in doubt as to whether or not you would be welcome, just ask someone, but do not feel hesitant just because you were not specifically invited. If it is a cooperative party, do your share of the work and participate in the fun, too. Sometimes these events are "potluck," meaning everyone brings a dish or two to add to the food being served; sometimes there is a charge to participate; sometimes everything is free.

When to Arrive and Leave

For Meals. You should arrive at the time indicated in the invitation or within five to ten minutes of that time. If you are very early, walk around the block or wait in your car or downstairs in the lobby. In this country the host and/or hostess are also likely to be the cooks. Give them time to do last-minute preparations; don't arrive before the time you were asked for. On the other hand, if you find you are going to be more than twenty to thirty minutes late, it is a courtesy to your host and hostess if you telephone and tell them so. They may turn off the stove and be grateful to you for not having spoiled supper by your lateness.

For Cocktail Parties, Receptions, Teas. Invitations for formal events usually say "from X hour to Y hour"—5:00 P.M. to 7:00 P.M., for example. This means that you can come any time that suits you between those hours. You do not have to leave exactly at the time indicated, but you should go within a half hour of the end at the latest. Following the example of the other guests is a good policy for newcomers.

For a Dance. Most people arrive thirty minutes to an hour after a dance starts. There is nothing more dreary than a dance that has not yet gotten under way, unless you are a true dancer who likes the floor uncrowded and the orchestra fresh.

For Concerts and the Theater. Plan to arrive at least ten minutes before curtain time, or much earlier if the event is by "general seating," which means that no seats are assigned ahead of time. You will want to take off your coat, read the program, and settle down before the play begins. In many theaters and concert halls, if you are late you will not be seated until the first break in the program.

For Weddings, Funerals, Public Lectures, Sports Events. Be there about ten minutes before the specified time so that you will be seated and relaxed by the time it starts. In some cases you will want to arrive earlier to get a good seat.

For Business Appointments. Arrive exactly at the moment of appointment or a few minutes ahead. It is considered a discourtesy to keep a busy person waiting. If he or she keeps you waiting, however, try not to show impatience. The person whose office is the scene of the meeting takes precedence. If you do not want to give him or her this advantage, arrange to meet in your office or on some neutral ground such as at a club or in a hotel lobby.

Drinking

Drinking habits vary widely among Americans. Some families never serve any alcoholic beverages. Others have cocktails before dinner, wine with the meal, and/or after-dinner drinks. If you are not accustomed to American cocktails, be cautious; they are often quite strong. Women as well as men drink alcohol, but you should not feel any hesitation in asking for a sherry, Dubonnet, or nonalcoholic drink (such as Coca-Cola or fruit juice) if you do not want a cocktail. In some homes the cocktail hour may become quite lengthy. If it does and you do not wish to drink additional cocktails, it is perfectly all right to refuse. You can also drink as slowly as you like. Eating some of the food which is offered with the drinks is a good idea; there are usually cheese and crackers, olives, peanuts, potato chips with creamy "dips," or other small snacks.

If the host asks, "What will you have to drink?" you can reply, "What are you serving?" or you may request a particular drink if you prefer.

Common cocktails offered in most homes include:

- *Gin and tonic:* a particularly popular summer drink made with gin, quinine water, and ice—often with a sprig of mint and a slice of lemon or lime.

- *Scotch or bourbon:* two types of whiskey, served with water or with soda or "on the rocks." This last phrase means simply that liquor is poured over ice with nothing added. You can ask for "on the rocks with a little water" if you want it somewhat less strong.

- *Martini:* colorless but powerful; made with dry vermouth and gin, served either on the rocks or "straight up," meaning no ice is included. Served with a twist of lemon or an olive. You may also ask for a vodka martini.

- *Manhattan:* sweet and dark-colored, made with sweet vermouth and whiskey, served either on the rocks or straight up.

- *Bloody Mary:* a mild drink, often offered before lunch or at brunch, made of spiced tomato juice with a "shot" (one to two ounces) of vodka or gin, served over ice.

- *Screwdriver:* vodka and orange juice, also often offered at brunch. Some people drink these for cocktails, served over ice.

Drinks served on the rocks are not quite as strong as drinks served straight up, especially after the ice has melted a bit. Americans use more ice than almost anyone else in the world.

Many people prefer beer or wine instead of a cocktail, and most homes that serve cocktails also have beer and wine available. You can ask for white wine or red wine when the host asks you what you would like.

When office colleagues stop for a drink together on their way home, the one who made the suggestion often pays for the first drink; the companion frequently offers to pay for a second. This is no hard-and-fast rule, though; they may each pay for their own. Normally, if someone says, "How about a drink?" each pays his or her own bill. Many people have a drink over a business lunch.

If you do not want to do this, you can certainly decline. Beer or wine are also often ordered at lunch.

Do not be surprised if you are offered coffee, tea (iced or hot, depending on the season), or even Coca-Cola with a meal. Water is not always served, but feel free to ask for it in either a home or a restaurant.

Dinner in a Home

Dinner with Americans in their homes is likely to be informal and relaxed. You will probably be served family style. Platters and bowls will be passed from person to person, or the host may serve from one end of the table. All ages eat together. There is no clear division of labor in many modern American families. Serving cocktails, preparing dinner, clearing dishes from the table after the meal, washing dishes or putting them in the dishwasher—any of these chores might be done by one person or by several members of the family. Whether or not you help with any of these chores will vary depending on your rank and age, how often you have been to the home, and family custom. If you are a homestay student or a long-term visitor, you will come to be treated as part of the family and will participate in these responsibilities. If you are a visiting businessperson or executive or special guest, you will not be expected to participate.

At meals, it is the custom to wait for the host to begin eating and to finish as closely as you can to when everyone else does. Watch your host from time to time to judge your own speed. Americans tend to eat rather more quickly than many other people; you may be embarrassed if you find yourself far behind everyone else at the end of the meal.

If for religious (or other) reasons there are some foods you cannot eat, explain in advance to your host when the invitation is extended. You may say, "I should tell you that I do not eat pork for religious reasons," or "I'm on a rather restricted diet on the advice of my doctor, who tells me I shouldn't eat meat," or "I'm a vegetarian, and I hope this doesn't cause you any inconvenience." If you were unable to explain in advance, you can do so after you are at the table and see that there is something you shouldn't eat, or you can just leave it on your plate uneaten. Even though at first American food may be different and you may not enjoy it, it will please your host if you eat at least some of every dish and express appreciation for the effort. The cook (or cooks, since both husband and wife may have participated) in the family will probably have tried very hard to please you.

The American habit of shifting the fork from right to left hand when the knife is used—then back again—is unfamiliar to many. Don't feel you must struggle with this awkward custom. Do whatever is comfortable for you. It is *not* considered correct, though, to soak up gravy with bread, to tuck your napkin under your chin, or to make any kind of slurping, burping, or other noises while eating at the table, although some Americans do these things. Watching your host is a good idea! (See also "American Food Habits," pages 116-17.)

Buffet Meals

Buffet meals are a popular means of entertaining because they are informal and easy to manage, even without household help. There are no exact rules about what is proper; your host will indicate how people should proceed and where they are to sit. You can probably figure out what to do by watching other guests. Systems vary from household to household, depending on the way the house is arranged, how many people there are, and so on. Often, folding snack tables are provided; if you find it difficult to balance your plate or cut your meat, don't hesitate to seek out the corner of a more solid table and pull your chair up to it so that you are comfortable. Nobody will mind. The point is for people to feel at ease and to have a pleasant, relaxed time together.

You will naturally thank a host as you leave, but if you want to be considered really polite and pleasant, send a note within a day or two after the event. This will be greatly appreciated. If you prefer, you can express your thanks by telephone instead. This should be done on the day immediately following the party. Not everyone does this, but it is not difficult, and the host family will remember your gesture for a long time.

Bringing Gifts

Bringing flowers or a gift when you are invited for lunch or dinner is always welcome and gracious, especially when you first visit and on special occasions such as a birthday or Christmas. We go in and out of each other's houses so informally and so often, however, that gifts are by no means an obligation. If you do bring something, it should be small and simple—a gesture rather than a gift—perhaps a bottle of wine, a souvenir from your country, a small box of candy, an inexpensive bouquet of flowers, or something equally modest. If you are going to be an overnight or weekend guest, it is customary to bring a present, still not elaborate but more special than a gift brought for only a meal.

Sharing Household Tasks

Many families do not permit guests to do any work on the first visit, but if they become frequent guests in the house, then they gradually join in with the various household chores. Some people never let a guest help. It is a good idea to offer, but then act according to the response.

Men do a good deal more around an American house than is true in many parts of the world, especially if both husband and wife have full-time jobs. Either sex does whatever needs doing in many households—including caring for the baby, taking out the trash, and washing dishes. Men usually cut the grass and take care of major outdoor jobs, women often do the shopping, but it could be the other way around in some households. In other words, there is no clear-cut distinction between husband and wife concerning domestic responsibilities.

Relationships between Men and Women

Women's equality with men is a sensitive issue in the United States. Almost 60 percent of women of employment age are working, and they play prominent roles in business, political, social, educational, and community affairs. Women who work outside the home are demanding equality with men in terms of both responsibility and salary, but there is still a long way to go. Women in the professions, in offices, in shops, in factories, in all sorts of jobs often receive salaries well below those of men for the same job.

Some married American women choose to be housewives. In today's world, taking care of all the tasks of managing a home and children is considered a vocation, and a few have even suggested that homemakers should be paid a salary just like women who choose to work outside the home.

In spite of the movement toward equality, many women still appreciate some traditional courtesies and will not be offended by them, and many men still want to extend these courtesies to women. In most cases, men may still open doors for women and stand back to allow them to go through first. Women in the United States usually walk ahead of men into a room or theater or restaurant.

Americans are still trying to work out the meaning of equality between the sexes, and some men are confused about the changing roles or even threatened by women who are assertive and who hold administrative and executive positions. This is a difficult time for men who have traditionally felt that they should be breadwinners and women should be homemakers. In general, however, a cultural adjustment is taking place, and most people realize that men and women can actually get along on an equal footing with one another.

Safety and Unescorted Women

Women who are alone are far more free here than in many parts of the world; one sees unescorted women almost anywhere. Unfortunately, however, crime is widespread here and certain precautions are necessary.

A woman can feel safe in planes, buses, and trains (day or night). It is safe for a woman to drive long distances alone if she wants to do so. Service station attendants and hotel and motel personnel will give friendly help; if there is trouble with the car along the way, a single woman will nearly always get help from passersby or the highway patrol. But if a woman (or a man, for that matter) is driving alone in a city, it is wise to keep the car doors locked and valuables out of sight. These two simple habits can prevent someone from jumping quickly into the car at a stop light or grabbing something through an open window.

Cities have become less safe after dark because an increasing number of people are turning to crime in search of money, often for drugs. The drug problem in the United States is serious and growing worse. Stay on well-populated and well-lit streets; do not walk in parks at night; take taxis after about 9:00 P.M. Hold your purse carefully, don't let shoulder bags hang loosely, and don't wear valuable jewelry until you reach your destination. With the high price of gold and gems, jewelry is a "hot" item among thieves.

It is best to ask locally which streets are safe and which are not. Looks can be deceiving; some dark areas can be safe; well-lit ones may be dangerous at quiet times (like Wall Street after the business world goes home). Visitors to the United States should be particularly careful about safety. Until you have been here for a while, you won't know how to judge whether a situation, a person, or a place is dangerous because you won't know how to "read" the clues.

A woman can go alone into a restaurant for breakfast, lunch, or dinner, but most usually avoid sophisticated, expensive restaurants in big cities or fancy nightclubs with floor shows and/or dancing. Single women usually avoid public bars unless they want to go to one of the many catering to singles, but they can go comfortably to cocktail lounges in hotels.

Generally, people get friendlier and more casual as you go farther and farther west in the United States and as you leave large cities. In today's world it is generally advisable for a single woman not to hold a sustained conversation with a single man who approaches her in any public place in one of the large cities. A few words and a smile are fine, but if a man pursues a conversation, he may well be looking for a "pickup," meaning an easy date for sex. Avoid letting him see or overhear your address or room number.

Single women are, of course, frequently asked out for dates. There is no reason why you cannot accept, and also return such invitations—inviting single men to your apartment for dinner or a party, either alone or in a group. An invitation to a single man for dinner or drinks in your apartment, however, is sometimes interpreted by the man as an invitation for sex as well.

Adult Dating

Men and women go out together a great deal, especially in the cities. They ski together, work together, and dine together, either at restaurants or in each other's apartments. A date does not mean that they are necessarily interested in having sex together, though it may appear so and, of course, with some men and women it is so.

To a male Arab, African, or Latino, or to many of the other men of the world, including some American men, the fact that a woman will readily go off alone with him often seems to imply that she is sexually available. This is not true. It is important to realize this from the start. You will scare off many American women if you rush in too fast; they may seem very friendly yet have no intention whatsoever of having sex with you at the first meeting or, for that matter, at any other time. Most American women are not promiscuous. They may choose to have sex, even extramarital sex, but generally not unless they feel real affection for the man; and most stay with one man at a time for considerable periods. Most are not looking for "an easy make" and do not appreciate the assumption that they are.

If you have a wife or husband at home, be sure to let this fact be known to your acquaintances early on. It will not necessarily make any difference, but the American wants to know the situation. She or he will feel tricked and will frequently cut off the relationship immediately if suspecting that the other has cheated, lied, or otherwise been misleading.

Single men dating American women should generally not make any move toward having sex on the first date. In today's world of free speech, though, you can ask a woman how she feels about having sex, but your chances will be poor if you move too fast too soon, regardless of how informal things may look here.

A woman will not feel that she owes you sex because you have paid for her dinner. She will feel that her company and her acceptance of you have contributed toward a pleasant evening for both but not that she owes you more. You have to achieve anything beyond a casual friendship by being the kind of person she likes and wants. You cannot buy sexual intimacy by offering her a meal or gifts as though she were a prostitute.

American women are accustomed to easy companionship and equality. Anyone who comes here expecting to find American women meek, obedient, or submissive is likely to have a hard time. Today's American woman is very much her own person: independent, and intending to stay so. She expects to make her own choices and expects decisions to be made jointly.

Who pays for dates? A general rule of thumb is that a woman in business or college will pay her own way during the day. If, however, a man asks her to something special outside normal working hours—for cocktails or dinner, a dance, or the movies—the invitation itself means "come as my guest." The whole matter of dating is in transition. Young men and women are quite open and candid in talking over who will pay and for what. You can feel quite free to ask your friends for advice in your situation.

Single women coming to a job in the United States will often have to work a bit at finding ways to meet men. Men in offices are likely to be family men who rush out at five o'clock to get back home to their wives and children. Single men often fear developing an intimate relationship with someone they will see and work with every day. There is also much discussion nowadays about sexual harassment in the workplace, as discussed elsewhere.

The best way for a single woman to meet men or other women easily is likely to be through sports activities or some kind of club. Go skiing or join a bowling team; play golf or tennis; take a membership in a swimming club. If you are not athletic, enroll in an evening class that appeals to both sexes—photography, ballroom dancing, judo, or computer programming, for instance. Select your hobby with a little thought!

If you are asked for a date, remember that you can set the pace. In this country the man generally does the inviting and the planning, but he is likely to find out first what will please his guest. You will probably have an opportunity to indicate the kinds of things you enjoy: mountain climbing or listening to music, being with a group or eating alone together by candlelight. In addition to choosing along such lines, it is you who also sets the level of friendship. You can keep things platonic if you want to. If the man seems increasingly affectionate and you want it to be otherwise, you can make that clear. The woman has the choice.

Most big cities contain many single men and women who come from elsewhere to work. Since both find it hard to meet new people, many "singles clubs" have sprung up. These can be free-for-all places to pick up someone for sex, or they can be extremely nice clubs, offering theater parties, cocktail parties, and other activities to help men and women become acquainted. These organized clubs sometimes publish a monthly booklet or have a bulletin board describing the range of activities that will take place that month. If interested, you can go to whichever parties or events you choose. If you find congenial people of either sex, that is fine. If not, you may try again on some other occasion. There are always people at the door to introduce you and make it easy for you to meet and mix, even if you are alone.

Start slowly if you join such a group. Be a little reserved at first. The super-friendly type who rushes up to make friends may in fact be the club bore looking for a new audience. Give yourself time to look over the situation before you become too friendly with anyone. Clubs of this sort are often found through church contacts; otherwise, ask around or watch the local newspapers.

There are also a large variety of sports/exercise clubs that cater to men and women, married and single. These clubs can be a nonthreatening way to meet someone while doing something you like.

Personal ads, or "personals," have become a very popular way for single men and women to meet. It is particularly attractive to those for whom the club or bar scene isn't appealing.

Most daily and weekly newspapers as well as many magazines offer personals, with numerous formats and response set-ups. You may either respond to an ad or write your own. These services are usually quite reasonable compared with expensive dating services.

But *shopper beware!* Responding to personals can be dangerous, especially in large cities. Discuss this with colleagues or friends before taking any chances; there may also be some listings that are less risky than others. If you do decide to try your luck, always meet the other person during daylight hours and in a public place.

Alternative Lifestyles

In most cities there are bars and restaurants catering to gays and lesbians. Foreign visitors who are homosexual or bisexual may find listings in the telephone directory for a gay and lesbian community center or gay service center, which will provide information on local bars, organizations, or clubs. Also, one can often find newspapers and magazines in large bookstores which will list establishments catering to gays and lesbians.

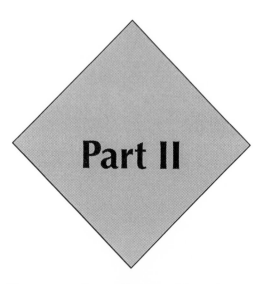

Part II

Practical Pointers

8

Clothes You Will Need

Winter temperatures throughout much of the country range from 0°F (or below) to about 65°F (-20°C to 18°C). One should also be prepared for a good deal of wind. For outdoor wear, heavy coats or down parkas with hoods, warm mittens or gloves, and a hat and scarf are essential in many places in the north because of the wind and cold. There is often snow, but in most cities it is quickly cleared, especially in the northernmost part of the country. In southern areas, the winter climate is much warmer.

Indoors, in winter, buildings are likely to be kept somewhere around 60°-68° or higher—much warmer than in Europe. You will need lightweight wool for winter, with additional sweaters, jackets, stoles, ponchos, or the like to put on or take off easily as you move from outdoors to indoors. Those who come from hot climates will perhaps feel the cold very much at first and should be prepared with layers, such as extra scarves or sweaters, and warm underwear.

You will also need a raincoat during the four in-between months of spring and autumn (April-May and September-October). The combination kind with removable zip-out lining is especially useful.

Americans in general like bright colors; dress is informal, even in the cities. Few women wear hats, for example, except during cold, windy weather or for very dressy occasions such as weddings. Dark business suits for men and cocktail dresses for women suffice at most evening functions. People rarely wear formal attire (tuxedos and long evening dresses) for the theater except on opening nights. If formal attire is required at a function or at someone's home, you will be told "black tie." This, too, is rare, even in large cities.

Children and teenagers dress very casually except for special occasions when they are dressed in party clothes. In some parochial schools and a small number of private schools, uniforms are required. A few schools still require jackets and ties for boys. In general, though, boys and girls generally wear a variety of sturdy and informal clothes to school, often jeans or corduroy slacks and T-shirts, sweatshirts, or sweaters. During the summer months children and teenagers often wear shorts and T-shirts to school. The trend for teenagers is increasingly individualistic—even bizarre. Dress-up occasions can be quite competitive, ranging anywhere from "doing your own thing" to formal dresses and suits, depending on the geography and on personal taste.

9

Moving around Your New City

Americans move around a city on foot or by bus, taxi, car, or (in some cities) subway (sometimes called the metro)—just as is done the world over in cities.

On Foot

If distances are short, the quickest way to go may be on foot. Traffic in our cities and towns is often very heavy, particularly during morning and evening rush hours at the beginning and ending of the workday. So city people often get to their destination most quickly on foot if distances permit. Many people also walk as a form of exercise.

Jaywalking, which means either crossing in the middle of a block or crossing against the traffic light, is illegal in most communities, and you could be fined if caught. You will see many people taking chances, but do not follow their example. It is not worth it. Most pedestrian injuries are the result of jaywalking.

If you come from a country where driving is on the left, be especially careful to look *both* ways for oncoming cars and have your children practice doing the same. Many people are hurt by failing to do this before stepping off the curb.

By Bus

Trams or trolley cars are now rarely found in U.S. cities; generally the public travels by bus. More and more cities are requiring passengers to have the exact change in hand as they board the bus—or else "tokens" (small coinlike pieces similar to the French *jeton*) that can be bought in advance. Drivers used to have the double job of making change at the same time that they were driving their huge buses through traffic. The exact-change rule eases the driver's work and speeds service for everyone. It also reduces the number of robberies that were taking place when drivers had a great deal of extra money for making change.

In many cities bus and subway tokens can be used interchangeably and are bought at subway booths. It is a great time-saver to buy tokens in considerable quantity and keep them in a special purse or envelope so that you can get at them easily. Otherwise, you may have to wait in long lines during rush hour or get caught without change just when you need to catch a bus. If you are using two buses (or a subway and a bus) to reach your destination, you can request a transfer that allows you to pay one fare for the entire trip but use two (or sometimes more) vehicles to complete your trip.

Bus stops are usually at busy corners and are clearly marked. Usually the bus schedule is displayed at the stop, and in most cities you can request printed bus schedules from the bus company. In some cities you can telephone to ask for the best route to go from one point to another. If time allows, the bus driver will often give quick directions or at least tell you when to get off the bus.

Schoolchildren and people over sixty-five years of age can get special passes in most cities so that they can ride at reduced rates during certain hours of the day.

By Subway (or Metro)

Subways or metros in some cities are by far the quickest way to move about. Networks of them lie under a number of our cities, operating day and night. Most of the time they are filled with people and can be used safely. There are a few warnings, however, that should be observed.

1. Naturally, avoid rush hours if you can. Subways are full from about 7:30 to 9:30 A.M. and again from about 4:30 to 6:00 or 6:30 P.M. (These are the hours when pickpockets do their best work, too.)

2. Choose to sit in cars where there are other people, rather than empty ones.

3. For safety while waiting for a train, stand near the token booth if possible.

4. Hold your purse firmly and consciously—don't let it dangle. Men should carry wallets in inside jacket pockets.

5. Save yourself trouble by buying tokens in quantity if you plan to use subways regularly.

6. Before riding the subway at night, ask a friend or colleague whether it is safe and whether there are areas of the city that should be avoided at night.

Subway or metro stops are clearly marked, and maps of the system are available at most stations. In some systems, tickets that are purchased from a machine are used rather than tokens. The machine takes coins and bills and gives change.

By Taxi

Because at first they feel uncertain, most people are likely to travel by taxi when they arrive in any new place. Here, taxis definitely come under the heading of luxury travel. In Chicago or New York, for example, the meter reads $1.00 or more before you even move! Furthermore, taxis have an aggravating way of being hard to find, not only at the busy hours of a day but also if the weather turns bad.

In most cities you can telephone to get one (see the local phone book for numbers); but in others, including New York, you usually hail them on the street or find them at a "hack stand" (special parking areas reserved for taxis).

Generally speaking, taxis are metered throughout the country, but there are some cities (for example, Washington, D.C.) where they operate on a distance zone system. Nothing is uniform in the United States. You will need to ask a friend, a colleague, or hotel personnel about the rules; they vary from city to city. Also be sure to use a well-known taxi company to avoid being overcharged.

Although drivers do not always comply, the regulations are as follows: They must stop if the taxi is empty and not showing an off-duty sign; they must drive anywhere within the city limits; they may not ask your destination before you get in and then refuse to take you. They may not charge more than is registered on the meter except for trunks, for bridge, tunnel, or ferry tolls, or for late-night special fees. Off-duty signs are often indicated by lights on the taxi roof, but it is wise to ask someone how to tell when a taxi is off duty and can therefore be expected to pass you by. It varies from city to city.

There are various sizes of cabs. Often they are not permitted to carry more than four people—sometimes as few as three—but some can carry five or six passengers. If you find yourself sharing a cab with several strangers (legal in some cities but not in others), you will often be expected to pay full price, unfair though that may seem.

In heavily congested areas the driver may not be allowed by law to get out of the cab to open doors or help with luggage. Do not assume the driver is being discourteous—it may be a safety measure.

If you want to make a complaint about taxi service, note the driver's number and name (posted somewhere inside the cab). Be sure to get the name of the taxi company also—there are many companies in all cities. When you write to the company, be sure to keep a copy of your letter.

By Car

Costs

Owning a car in any U.S. city is expensive. In addition to the original cost of the car, one has to pay heavy insurance premiums. Rates vary by city and by coverage, but one can pay substantial amounts in insurance alone in congested cities. In addition, the car must be registered and licensed (fee depends on the weight or type of car). The cost of a driver's license must be added to that. The price of gasoline hardly needs comment, and parking costs are often *very* high, particularly in large cities.

There are no customs or other duty charges on a private imported car if it is shipped home again within one year; however, if you sell it in the United States within a year, you will have to pay duty—based on the appraised value of the car at the time of import. Be *sure* to bring your registration papers or proof of ownership. This is very important. Check with your nearest U.S. consulate or with your local automobile club on the latest rulings and charges before you come. There are also strict regulations regarding the pollution emissions of cars. Your car will have to be adapted to conform to these rules. This can be prohibitively expensive for foreign cars.

In many states, a car tax is added to the registration fee (done once a year), the amount dependent on the age and make of the car. Also, most states require an inspection once a year or every six months to determine that the car is safe to drive.

Licensing

If you bring your car, it is recommended that you get an international registration marker for it before leaving home. You will be allowed to drive to your destination with your national license plates or tags, but immediately on arrival you must obtain American license plates from the state in which you will be living. Each state has its own Department of Motor Vehicles (see telephone directory for address) which issues both license and registration. Motorists will have to take a test and secure a U.S. driver's license unless they come from a country which is party to the International Convention on Road Traffic (1949) or the Inter-American Convention (1943), in which case they must carry an international driving permit. If you buy a car in the United States, you must obtain a driver's license for the state where you live within a set time. And if you move to another state, you must do the same. Since regulations are complicated and vary somewhat from state to state, play it safe and call the Department of Motor Vehicles in your town or city to inquire about licensing and license plates. It is also wise to have at least a few hours of professional instruction *no matter how well you drive,* to learn rules of the road, local requirements, and, especially, American "driving psychology." Brazilian, Greek, Japanese, and French drivers are all different behind a wheel; so are Americans.

Each state's Motor Vehicle Bureau will give you a free booklet, upon request, covering state rules. It is important to remember: *Ignorance of the law is never considered an excuse* if you run into trouble. You are expected to learn the law and abide by it when you drive.

Automobile Insurance

It is imperative that you protect yourself with liability insurance (covering damage to the other person), and you should insure yourself at a substantial level, not the minimum. If you should hit someone, damages charged here can be astronomically high. Lawyers assume that insurance companies (not the individual) will pay, so they ask damage fees accordingly. If you are *not* covered, you can be financially ruined by gigantic fees charged for injury, fright, shock, or other complaints—even if the accident appeared to you to be slight. Not everyone presses such suits, but enough people do so that you need to be well protected. Although insurance is costly, it is absolutely necessary. Insurance premiums vary, depending on the age and sex of the driver, the type of car, and the geographic area; premiums for young, single men who own sports cars are extremely high.

Buying a Car

Barring any strikes or emergency delays, you receive delivery on a new car quite quickly in this country. American manufacturers are still building cars with high horsepower and low mileage per gallon of gas. Small cars, American- and foreign-made, are also very popular. In general, foreign cars are easy to obtain and to keep repaired, although repair and parts may be more expensive.

Don't buy a car at what is called "list price" until you have talked to a number of people about it. Prices can usually be bargained down and can vary considerably among dealerships. Prices also fluctuate markedly from one month to another, depending on how close it is to the appearance of new models. If you buy in the fall, just before the new models become available, dealers are trying to get rid of last year's model, and you can get a good bargain as a result. Ask and explore; don't buy too fast.

Car dealers make their greatest profit in two ways: (1) on extras and (2) on arranging the financing and insurance.

Extras. Extras are the multitude of optional features which all dealers try hard to sell: radios, cassette players, special paint color, air conditioning, fancy seat covers, and other items that are not standard. Dealers are skilled at selling these items, but *you do not need to buy them*. If you are persuaded by a clever salesperson, you may end up paying a considerable amount of money.

Financing and Insuring. Dealers normally charge higher interest rates than banks when they arrange the terms of financing. Over the months or years of payment, this can be a considerable amount. Look into alternative possibilities *before* you buy. Generally, you will do better to take out your own bank loan rather than work through a car dealer, who, after all, must take his or her share, and then work with a bank anyway. Dealers will do their best to persuade you to finance the car through them, but it is not required. Don't feel obligated.

Secondhand Cars

The drop in value of American cars after a year or two is so great that many people buy used cars rather than new ones. Prices depend on the age of the car, its condition, its size and make, the area of the country where it is bought, and the time of year.

> *Rule #1.* Be especially careful when buying a secondhand car that is older than four years.

> *Rule #2.* Never go alone. Take someone with you who not only knows cars well, but also knows the ways of American dealers.

Often it is an advantage to go to an area where wealthy people live to find your car. They turn their cars in more often than less affluent people, and the cars are normally in better condition.

Used-car dealers vary widely as to reliability; try to deal with one that has been recommended to you. Generally speaking, your chances will be better with a reputable dealer than at a used-car lot, though you will see a lot of these outside most big cities.

Many people do their buying outside city limits for a couple of reasons. The dealer's reputation is more vulnerable in a small town so he or she tends to be more careful than in the anonymity of a large city. Second, one can avoid paying city sales taxes. In New York City, for example, there is an 8 percent city sales tax added to the price of any purchase. If you can avoid this by going outside the city, your savings may be considerable.

It takes time and trouble to buy a secondhand car. If you do not have a friend or colleague who knows cars well, take a garage mechanic with you. It would be worth what you have to pay him for his time. Many mechanics are glad to do such consulting work after hours or on weekends. Determine the price of this service in advance, however.

Be sure you actually *drive* the car before buying. You will be allowed to do so. If you haven't brought a mechanic with you, take the car immediately to a nearby garage and ask the mechanic to test it out and give you an opinion as to its condition. There are certain key points he will look for that will give him a quick idea of the car's general condition. It is worth paying something for a careful examination by a mechanic whom you trust. Do this *before* you sign any papers. Before you buy any car—new or used—talk to people at your office or college or to any friends you have made. There are various tricks of the trade that you should know.

Leasing a Car

Leasing has become quite popular in the United States. It can be a particularly attractive option if you plan to live in the United States for only a few years and don't want the trouble of having to sell a car before you leave. Typically, leases last for two to three years, during which you make monthly payments. At the end of the lease, you simply return the car to the original dealer with no remaining obligations. Lease rates tend to be high, though, and most dealers require you to carry extra insurance.

Leasing has one major drawback. If you decide you don't want to keep the car for the duration of the lease and return it early, you may be obligated to pay the dealer the difference in the value of the car from the date you first leased it to the date you return it. This can sometimes add up to thousands of dollars. If you're sure you will keep the car for a set period of time, however, a lease is an option to consider.

Renting a Car
With street parking so difficult, parking rates so high, and streets so crowded, increasing numbers of city dwellers find owning a car in the city not worth the effort. Instead, they use public transportation within the city and rent a car only when they need one for out-of-town trips or vacations. Most overseas visitors are likely to find this by far the cheapest and easiest method, too. There are many rental companies everywhere. One can rent by the day, week, month, or year.

If you work in the United States your own firm may have a special discount arrangement with a particular rental agency—companies often do. It is worth asking about this at work. Some agencies have had bad experiences and will not rent to individuals from abroad because of past insurance difficulties or problems with payments. On the other hand, other agencies give additional discounts to visitors from abroad as a special courtesy. You will need to explore a bit and make inquiries.

Costs are usually determined by length of rental time and size of car. Insurance is extra. However, there are other options: Some agencies also charge by mileage, others do not; some require that you return the car to its starting point, others will rent cars for one-way travel between cities, although the cost for one-way rentals may be considerably higher.

Driving While Drunk

The United States is trying to stop drunken driving—as are many other countries. State laws vary on this, but police can stop drivers and make them take breath or blood tests in many states if they suspect the driver of being under the influence of alcohol. Penalties vary from state to state—fines for a first offense, overnight or longer imprisonment, suspension of license, or, in some areas, required community service (working as assistants in hospitals or nursing homes, for instance) or alcohol counseling.

Theft of Cars and from Cars

Unfortunately, car theft is quite common. You can expect little sympathy if your car was not locked or if the key was left in the ignition. The registration papers and your driver's license should be kept with you and not in the glove compartment, where they would be convenient for the thief but not for you when trying to recover a stolen car! Many people keep photocopies of these papers in the car.

Care should be taken regarding any possessions left in the car. If you must leave something, put it in the trunk or out of sight on the floor, even if the car is locked. If you are traveling across the country in a loaded car, try to park it where you can see it when you stop for meals. At night take all visible items with you into your motel or hotel. Put the rest in the locked trunk.

Gasoline and Service Stations

Cars are now made to take only unleaded gasoline. Leaded gasoline pollutes the air and can cause lead poisoning, especially in small children.

Prices vary by company and by area or state, depending on local taxes, but in general gasoline in the United States is cheaper than in most countries of the world. You can pay with cash or credit card. In some areas of the country, a small discount is offered on cash payment. The U.S. gallon is approximately four liters according to the metric system (slightly smaller than the British imperial gallon).

Free services which one can ask for at full-service stations include checking the oil and tires and cleaning the windshield. One does not tip gas station attendants for any of these services. At full-service stations or aisles, one can order gas by asking for a specific number of gallons, by price ("eight dollars worth, please"), or by asking to have the tank filled up. Most tanks hold from ten to twenty gallons when full.

Most stations have "self-service" pumps where motorists put in their own gas at a reduced price and forego other services. Anyone can use the restrooms, though frequently you must ask for the key from the attendant.

If your engine is hot, the attendant should not be asked to check the water in your radiator and may decline to do so. So many attendants have been badly burned by gushing steam and water that this is no longer a regular service.

Traffic Rules

Cars travel on the right throughout the United States. One must by law signal not only for all turns but also for lane changes. Traffic laws are being enforced more and more strictly as congestion problems grow ever more acute in American cities and on the highways. Police may travel in unmarked cars, and speed is often checked by radar. If you hear the sirens of fire trucks, ambulances, or police cars approaching, *immediately* pull over to the right and stop or slow down to let them pass.

Horn blowing is not appreciated and is prohibited in some cities; don't try to move traffic along by using your horn. You could be fined and you will attract the anger of other motorists.

If you come to a yellow school bus at a standstill and with flashing red lights, even if it has stopped on the opposite side of the road, you must *stop your car*. This law is strictly enforced because children may be running across the road to or from the bus.

Never stop your car on a highway. If you have a problem or want to read a map or change drivers, drive the car (or push it) well to the side of the road and switch on the emergency lights. Speeds on our highways are so fast that a stopped car is extremely dangerous, for oncoming drivers cannot see that it is stationary until they are too close to stop or swerve to avoid a collision.

Never pass on a curve or near the top of a hill; don't ever cross solid yellow or white lines, double or single. These are among the most common offenses police look for. They also watch for anyone going through a red light or a stop sign at an intersection or making a U-turn on a highway. In some states you can turn right on a red light if you are in the outside lane; in others, you cannot. Also, some intersections are marked "no right turn on red." One can be stopped and fined for any of these faults.

Traffic lights are controlled for different speeds; in large cities these vary depending on the area, flow of traffic, and time of day. Often they are set for twenty-five miles per hour. If you try to find and maintain the set speed, you will "make" most lights and flow with the traffic. Talk to taxi drivers about this. They are experts at "making lights" and can give you many tips.

Speed Limits

Although one sees people driving at high speeds, speed limits *can* be strictly enforced—by radar, by police helicopters, by unmarked police cars, and sometimes by regular police cars which radio to one another up and down the highways.

Watch all road signs carefully as you drive along. Speed limits change frequently at various locations. *Do what they say.* They may decrease suddenly, for example, at the approach to a small town or built-up area, a factory roadway, or a railroad. They are particularly enforced in school traffic zones, which extend on either side of any school and are posted as "School Zone." This is usually posted at fifteen miles per hour; it is essential to reduce speed drastically in such zones. Small children may cross the road by themselves on their way to or from school; they may also play and ride bicycles along the edge of the road and therefore create a hazard.

Parking Rules

When you park a car, read the signs carefully. Parking regulations vary in different parts of the city, at different times of the day, on different days of the week, or at different seasons of the year. The only way you can know what is legal for that particular spot is to read the sign. Many cars are towed away each day by city police for parking violations. It is not worth the risk to disobey the rules. You must pay the tow-away cost, expenses for actually retrieving your car, and a heavy penalty fine for parking illegally in the first place. The whole thing can add up to several hundred dollars. In addition you go through endless red tape, embarrassment, and inconvenience. Be careful not to park near fire hydrants, bus stops, or private driveways, nor too near the corner at intersections. Being towed away can result from any of these parking violations, as well as for being in a "no parking" area. In cities where it snows during the winter, signs are often posted for snow removal after a storm. Do not park on a street so posted.

The following are some common parking rules:

No stopping: This means what it says: You cannot park or even stop.

No parking: Here you may stop long enough to pick up or discharge passengers or to drop off merchandise. You can stop your car for a brief time if someone stays in the driver's seat and is able to move the car if necessary.

No standing: You may only drop people off or pick them up if you can do it quickly. You cannot wait for anyone and you cannot leave the car there while you go in to deliver a parcel or message.

Fire hydrants: The rule is no standing or parking within fifteen feet.

Bus stops and taxi stands: If you do not interfere with traffic, you can pause briefly, but you cannot get out of the car. You must be able to move at a moment's notice.

Hitchhikers

You will sometimes see people of either sex "thumbing" a ride, especially along the main highways. *Do not* stop for them. Unfortunately, this practice can be quite dangerous, as they may not be as innocent as they look. Furthermore, in many states it is as illegal to pick up a person as it is to ask for rides. You can be fined quite heavily and lose your insurance for doing it. Most certainly, *do not* try to hitchhike yourself!

Finding Restrooms

A newly arrived visitor from Scotland was asked what had been the most difficult thing for him on his first day in the United States. Without a moment's hesitation, he answered, "Finding a men's room."

Some countries have public restrooms plainly visible on the street or in small buildings that are clearly marked. The United States does not. Americans find facilities in such public places as restaurants, libraries, museums, or department stores. Reasonably clean restrooms are available at most gasoline stations, but toilets at bus terminals or railroad stations are often unpleasant, and restrooms in subway stations are often unsafe.

You can always go into a hotel and use the facilities, whether or not you are registered there as a guest; you will usually find them somewhere off the main lobby.

Don't be confused by the name on the door. Sometimes it is marked "Men" or "Women," sometimes "Gentlemen" or "Ladies," or there may be no word used at all, just a picture of a woman or a man or some other clue painted on the door. The European terms "Comfort Station" or "W.C." are not used. If you are in need, just ask for the "Men's Room" or "Ladies' Room."

In a large hotel or restaurant, leave a tip in the small saucer if there is an attendant—fifty cents is common. One does not tip in clubs, but a smile and a friendly word are appreciated. In some public restrooms there may also be some "pay toilets," although these have been abolished by law in most states. A coin must be inserted in the door to unlock it so you may enter.

10

Managing Money

Coins and Bills

American money can be quite confusing. U.S coins are as follows: 1 cent (penny), 5 cents (nickel), 10 cents (dime), and 25 cents (quarter). You may occasionally find a fifty-cent coin (half dollar), but there are very few still in circulation. All coins are silver-colored except for the penny, which is copper-colored.

One has to keep considerable change on hand, especially in cities which require exact change for buses. Bus drivers are not allowed to make change in many cities. You may have to buy tokens for bus travel. Ask where to do this, as it varies by city. Sales tax requires small coins, although stores will make change if needed.

Bills, or paper money, are all the same color and size. One has to look carefully to be sure one is using a $1 bill and not a $10 bill, for example. Bills that you are likely to use come in the following denominations: $1, $5, $10, $20, $50, and $100. The $50 and $100 bills are not carried by many people. Keep small-value bills with you. Taxi drivers, subway attendants, and some store clerks will not change anything larger than a twenty-dollar bill; most supermarkets and large department stores will, however.

It is a good idea to get a selection of American coins and bills from your bank before leaving home and practice with them so that you can recognize them easily. If you do this with your children, too, they can also become comfortable with the currency before they even arrive.

There is no limit to the dollars you may bring into or take out of the United States; however, your own country may restrict the amount you are allowed to take with you. You will need to check on that before leaving home.

Money on Arrival

You should have with you a minimum of fifty to one hundred dollars in American currency on arrival at a U.S. airport, for tips to porters and for transportation into the city. There are money exchanges in all international airports, but it is a bother to stop at the moment of arrival when you also have to cope with luggage, crowds, and fatigue. It is better to convert an adequate supply of money before departing. Taxi fares are rising rapidly in this country, and airports are generally several miles outside the city. Airport buses are much less expensive and are recommended unless you have a large number of people in your group or considerable luggage. A bus will take you to a central point in the city from where you can hire a cab to your final destination at far lower cost. Ask about them at the information desk at the airport. Many large hotels provide their own transportation (shuttle) to and from the airport; hotel guests may ride free of charge.

Banks

You may find that banks in the United States operate quite differently from banks in your country. Before you open a checking or a savings account, ask a bank officer about the various checking and savings plans and the rules and regulations regarding such features as required balances, purchasing checks, ATM (automated teller machine) cards, overdrafts, and making deposits. The banking business has become very competitive, so you may find a large, and sometimes confusing, array of accounts available. The ones described here are available in most banks but may be listed under different names.

Some checking accounts require a specific balance (usually between $100 and $500), called a "minimum daily balance," in the bank at all times, but there is no charge for each check issued and no monthly service fee if the balance does not drop below the minimum daily balance. Other accounts, called by various names at different banks, do not require as large a balance, but there is a charge for each check and sometimes a monthly service charge as well. There are also special accounts for larger balances. Banks charge service fees for falling below the required minimum and penalties for "bounced" checks (checks not covered by sufficient funds). Most banks allow you to combine a savings and checking account—and earn interest on the money that would usually be in the checking account. These are worth investigating; you should compare what is offered by different banks and try to choose a bank that is convenient for you to visit.

Take Care with Cash

However much money you keep in your home or in your wallet or purse, be extremely careful with it. Never leave a wallet or purse on a desk in your office or on a store counter *for even a moment*, and don't leave your purse in a supermarket basket. At home keep it out of sight and away from the entrance, and do not carry too much cash when you go out. Regretfully, purse snatching and pocket picking are quite common in metropolitan areas in the United States, as they are in other parts of the world.

Safe Deposit Boxes

If you have jewelry or other valuables (passports, wills, stock certificates, mortgage or insurance papers, leases, and so on), you should rent a safe deposit box at a nearby bank. This will cost between $15-$250 per year, depending on the size of the box and the area of the country. You can get your valuables out any time during banking hours, and these irreplaceable items will be safe and protected in bank vaults. If you are staying in a hotel, have the desk clerk put jewelry and other items into the hotel safe. *Do not leave valuables in your hotel room*, even in a suitcase. Insure expensive or irreplaceable jewelry, furs, cameras, watches, or other items that can easily be stolen. It is worth the cost and the extra time.

Sending Money Abroad

There are several ways to send money to someone in another country. If time is important, you may make arrangements at your bank by asking them to send a "wire transfer" to a bank in another country. If there is no urgency, banks can make less expensive transfers by letters to foreign banks. If you want the bank to notify the receiver of the funds, be sure to tell them the person's address. In order to receive such funds, the person will have to present him- or herself at the overseas bank with proper identification.

Money can also be sent abroad through the U.S. Postal Service (see chapter 13).

Charge Accounts and Credit Cards

The United States is becoming more and more a cashless society. People are making purchases by check, charge account, or credit card rather than carrying much money in their pockets or purses.

Most people receive monthly statements of bills and then send payment by check for charges such as department store purchases, telephone, electricity, gas, newspaper delivery, and similar household expenses. Many use credit cards to pay for gasoline and service station expenses and for restaurant, hotel, and travel costs. In most supermarkets a variety of payment options are available: cash, personal check, credit card, or bank card.

Many other people, however, prefer not to accumulate monthly bills. These people work out a combination, paying some bills in cash and charging others. This is a matter of personal choice. If you use credit cards, be sure to pay promptly; the interest charged for late payments can be high and your credit rating can be adversely affected if you do not pay your bills regularly.

Most credit card companies charge a yearly fee and an interest rate that varies from one company to the next. It is important to check the amount of the interest rate as well as the amount of the yearly fee; then select a card that costs you the least. Competition among credit card banks and companies is tremendous. Take your time in choosing a card, and read the information provided very carefully. Some companies advertise that they charge no yearly fees and some seem to be offering low interest rates on the amount carried over on the card, but buyer beware! Read the small print; most of these great deals are not deals at all. The most common credit cards are Visa, MasterCard, American Express, and Discover (which has no yearly fee). These cards can be used at most stores, restaurants, and hotels. Some stores, however, do not accept American Express. When you receive your credit card, be sure to sign the back of it in the space provided.

Most department stores offer charge accounts; they will ask for bank and other credit references. The process of opening an account may take a number of weeks. When your application is approved, you will be sent a credit card (sometimes called a "charge card") that can be used *only in that particular department store*. Charge cards greatly speed up the buying process. In addition, you can return goods and obtain a credit on your account (you generally will not get a cash refund).

The disadvantage to a credit or charge card is that one must be very careful with it. If you lose it and someone picks it up, or if someone steals your wallet, he or she can run up heavy charges on your account. If this happens to you, call the store or credit card service *immediately* and report the loss. Then *write them at once* and tell them again the day and time you phoned in to report the loss. Keep a copy of the letter. You will not be liable *after the time you first reported it.* Some people carry their credit cards only when they go shopping; others carry them whenever they go out, but whatever you do, always be on guard for possible purse snatchers or pickpockets.

ATMs are fast replacing bank services for withdrawing and, in some cases, even depositing money. When using an ATM, if possible, do so from a car—for safety reasons. When on foot, use normal safety precautions and be sure that no one sees you enter your PIN (personal identification number).

Tipping

Some people from other countries—and also many in the United States—oppose tipping, considering it undemocratic and demeaning. Furthermore, it is illogical—some people are tipped, like waiters and porters, and others, such as airline attendants, store clerks, and insurance agents, are not. Many feel that people should receive an adequate salary rather than tips.

However one feels about this, the fact is that in the United States many people do depend to a large extent on tips for their livelihood. In some fields of work, wages are simply not adequate. The theory is that by compensating people through tips rather than on a straight salary, you encourage good service. Although that is debatable, the system prevails.

One does not *have* to tip. If you are dissatisfied with service, you can show it by reducing or withholding a tip. But generally speaking, tipping is expected in the United States. It is a way of saying thank you to people who provide services for you.

People You Do Tip in the United States

Waiters, taxi drivers, porters, doormen, hat-and-coat-check attendants, and delivery people should all be tipped. You also tip for personal services from barbers, shoeshiners, hair stylists (or beauticians), and so on. Parking lot attendants should be tipped only if they have parked your car or brought it for you.

Unfortunately, many employers of these workers underpay, considering tips to be part of the wages. If you do not tip, therefore, you are depriving the worker of needed income.

People You Do Not Tip

1. *Customs officials or other government employees, such as police officers or firefighters*. This is considered bribery.

2. *Postal employees*. Although mail deliverers are not tipped,

often people give them a Christmas gift of five to ten dollars. The same goes for newspaper deliverers.

3. *Airline flight attendants or ticket agents.*

4. *Room clerks or people at hotel desks* (unlike the European concierge system).

5. *Bus drivers.* If, however, they also serve as guides on guided tours, then give them a dollar and thank them as you leave.

6. *Store clerks.*

7. *Gas station attendants.*

8. *Elevator operators, receptionists, or telephone operators.*

9. *Employees in private clubs.*

10. *Theater ushers or movie ushers.*

Normal Tips

Tipping customs and amounts vary considerably from one part of the United States to another, as well as from small towns to large cities. When you are settled in your area, you should ask about this locally.

To put newcomers at ease during their initial few days, the following guidelines are offered.

Porters. A dollar per bag is customary. Some people tip more if the bags are heavy and difficult to handle.

Taxi Drivers. The driver will expect 15 to 20 percent. If there are several of you, or if you have a lot of luggage, give at least 20 percent. In some cities there is an extra charge for each passenger. Such variations are posted in the cab.

Waiters. Give at least 15 percent to the waiter. A service charge is generally not included in the bill. Give the waiter more if you are particularly satisfied with the service, have asked for extras, had a large group, or requested help in understanding the menu or in serving young children; in other words, if you have received more than normal service. If you are part of a group of six or more, a 15 percent gratuity is generally added to your bill.

As everywhere, tips are naturally higher in finer restaurants. In such a place your tip for the waiter should not be less than 20 percent. If you order wine, the wine steward may expect a tip as well as the waiter.

In a low-priced snack bar or coffeehouse, the tip is about 10 percent, with a minimum of a quarter under your plate for just a cup of coffee or tea. If you order room service in a hotel, 15 to 20 percent of the bill is proper.

Doormen. For normal daily services, you do not tip except when they call a taxi. Then give them one dollar. If they help with a great deal of luggage at any time, give them one to three dollars, depending on the amount of trouble taken.

Most people give the doormen of their apartment houses occasional tips—ranging from one to five dollars—for any extra services they may perform, for special occasions, or for a good many small services done over a considerable length of time (that have gone untipped). This is not required, but it helps to keep service friendly and helpful.

Personal Services. It is hard to give a rule of thumb as to how much to tip barbers, hairdressers, delivery people, parking lot attendants, the maid who looks after your hotel room, and all such people who serve you. Rates vary, depending on the part of the country, how much service they have given, and other factors. The best advice is to ask locally, though if you ask four or five people in your office, at a party, or in your neighborhood about tipping, you will undoubtedly receive varied answers. If you cannot find anyone to ask easily, you can say directly to the person involved, "I would like to give you something for your service but I am a stranger here; what is the normal tip?" Almost surely you will get a big smile and an honest answer.

The Holidays. The winter holidays are special—and expensive. Here are some suggestions. If you live in an apartment house where there are doormen, give each one of them a gift of five dollars or more during the holidays. The amount will vary, depending on how long you have been living there, the size of your family, and how many other tips you have given throughout the year. Also, the superintendent of your apartment house should receive a gift of twenty dollars or more. If there are other service people such as trash collectors, porters, or telephone operators, you may also want to give them five dollars or so.

Holiday tips are sometimes given as well to the tradespeople one sees regularly—the laundry attendant, newspaper deliverer, parking lot attendant, hairdresser, or barber. These tips are flexible, depending on how often they have served you and on your financial situation. But if you feel friendly toward them, three to five dollars in a Christmas or Chanukah card would be much appreciated by any of these people who have worked for you throughout the year.

11

Medical Care

When people move to a new, unfamiliar country, they are often quite concerned about what might happen if they get sick. This is an understandable fear because medical practices and the customs that surround illness differ, sometimes dramatically, from culture to culture. Even if the medical care you receive is excellent, as it usually is in this country, there is still discomfort because it is not what you are accustomed to. The information below is intended to help you understand the practice of medicine in the United States so that you can obtain medical care with as little apprehension as possible.

Before You Leave Home

The first step to obtaining medical care in a new country is to bring your family's health records with you, if possible. This provides your new physician with a complete history of past medical experience and may help you save on expensive tests or background studies. Also, have all necessary dental work done before you leave home; costs for dental care in the States are as high as those for medical care.

If you wear eyeglasses or contact lenses, have an extra pair with you and be sure to bring a copy of the prescription. If you are on regular medication, it is a good idea to bring a copy of that prescription and information from your physician at home about the condition for which the medication is required.

Obtaining Medical Care

For general medical care, most people's primary doctor is a family practice specialist—someone who will provide routine care for all members of the family and who can refer you to other kinds of specialists when necessary. There are two kinds of specialists who are usually contacted immediately—a pediatrician if there is a young child in the family and a gynecologist for adult females. Many general practitioners, however, are qualified and experienced in treating children and gynecological matters as well.

Numerous medical groups have formed which give the patient access to a number of doctors rather than one. They emphasize family practice—taking care of all the medical needs of family members in one place and providing service at all times with one or another of the group members available on call. Many of these groups are referred to as Health Maintenance Organizations, or HMOs. Some are attached to hospitals but most are independent, and the physicians have privileges at local hospitals.

How do you go about finding a reliable doctor? Physicians are listed in the classified directory (often called the Yellow Pages), and many even advertise their services, but people usually find doctors by asking friends and acquaintances about their experiences with medical care. There are a variety of ways to search. Your company may advise you. Often there is a company doctor or an arrangement with a medical group. This is a great help. Perhaps you can ask your neighbors, or the person from whom you rent your apartment, or the head of your child's school. The officer at the bank or someone at your church, mosque, or synagogue may also give you advice. Your own consulate may have a list of doctors who speak your language.

Don't necessarily accept the first physician suggested. People have different needs. Most physicians are very well trained in the United States, so you rarely have to worry about technical competence. Probably the most important consideration, and one you can judge easily, is personality. You will want to find someone who is easy to talk with and in whom you have confidence. You may also want to inquire about costs if that is important to you.

If it is difficult to obtain a personal recommendation from someone you know, call the County Medical Society or the Physician Referral Service in your area. These offices can either provide a list of physicians or tell you where you can get this information. You can also call the administrator's office at the nearest hospital and ask for the names and office addresses of doctors with privileges at their hospital. This way you will find well-trained doctors with nearby hospital affiliations. Neither the hospital nor the County Medical Society will recommend one doctor; they will always provide several names. When you have been given the names and telephone numbers of several doctors, make an appointment with one of them. Take your family's health records and ask about fees, hospital connections, and anything else you want to know. If the doctor's age, medical training, and personality seem right to you, you will probably return whenever necessary. If not, you may want to look for another doctor.

Don't feel shy about discussing fees when you first make these contacts. They can vary and it is better to know in advance the approximate fees any given physician is likely to charge. Medical care is expensive in the United States and it is important to know what costs to expect.

Emergencies

If you have an emergency, the first step is to call your doctor. If you do not have a doctor—or if he or she is unavailable—go to the emergency room of the nearest hospital. Emergency rooms are set up to deal with serious accidents and acute illnesses (such as a heart attack). It is a good idea to find out where this facility is located before you need it. They are equipped to respond quickly to life-threatening situations. Less serious illnesses and accidents, although they may occur without warning, are treated by family physicians and in "walk-in" clinics. Some hospitals also have an "express care" service, separate from their emergency services.

In most of the country the emergency number for ambulance, police, or fire is 911, but it is wise to check this locally. If you do not know the emergency number, just dial "0" for the operator and tell the operator about your situation, but *do not forget to give your address and telephone number*. If you hang up without giving this critical information, you will have wasted precious moments while the operator tries to trace the call.

If You Are Sent to a Hospital

Although health care is expensive in the United States, it is good and in most cases very thorough. People are sent to hospitals more often here than in many other countries. If this happens to you, be sure you understand from the doctor exactly what the reason is before you become worried. It often means only that the doctor wants to make use of special facilities for tests, X rays, or treatment procedures or wants to have you observed at frequent intervals over a period of days by a trained staff. It does not necessarily mean that the doctor thinks you are seriously ill.

Health Insurance

Since medical costs are so high, insurance is necessary. There are many excellent free public facilities for the poor, but they are so crowded and the waiting time is so long that most people who can afford to, use private doctors. As of yet, there is no national system of health care coverage (except for Medicare, which covers persons sixty-five years of age and over), but the issue is hotly debated.

At the present time, the great majority of American people subscribe to private insurance programs, which help to pay for hospital and doctor bills. You should join such a program also. If you work for an American company, there is quite likely a group insurance plan to which you and your family will automatically belong, but you should find out about this in detail. Payments for such plans are made through automatic payroll deductions. Find out exactly what the coverage includes, since this varies from one plan to another. Also, check the deductible (the amount you must pay before the insurance covers the cost).

If you are working for an organization which does not have group insurance, you should purchase private health insurance for yourself and your family. One bad accident or serious illness could cost you a great deal of money. Most insurance plans are open to international personnel after they have lived in the United States for six months; a few will cover them earlier than that. Ask at your company about a good insurance adviser or ask your doctor. This needs to be done soon after arrival.

Foreign students enrolled in U.S. colleges and universities are usually required to have medical insurance (and J-1 students and scholars *must* have insurance). They also pay their college infirmary fee, which entitles them to receive full infirmary care whenever they need it. They can also purchase additional low-cost accident insurance, which is recommended—and often required. The university or college catalogue will give details, and the foreign student adviser will inform new students about the insurance plan recommended by the school. Dependent family members are often *not* eligible for infirmary care and should be covered with outside health insurance.

Medical insurance *almost never covers all expenses.* Read the policy carefully and have someone explain it to you in detail. Coverage varies widely from one policy to another. Some policies include prescription drugs and dental care, but few cover eyeglasses or doctors' visits to the home. You can have these specialties added, but the cost rises sharply with each one. Be sure to think over carefully exactly what you really need, balancing the cost of the policy against those services you can afford.

Before selecting a health insurance agent, it is a good idea to obtain advice from a colleague or friend. Most agents are reliable, but some are not; you will need help in selecting a reputable firm.

Paying Hospital Bills

Be prepared to pay all hospital bills before taking the patient home. Your corporation or your insurance may cover such matters for you; otherwise, the hospital may demand full payment—even if this requires your taking out a loan to cover it. It is advisable to talk to your employer, your doctor, or your insurance agent about this so you will know your own situation before an emergency arises. Occasionally, hospitals will agree to have payments spread over a period of time.

12

Food and Food Customs

Hotels

Most people start their visit to the United States by staying in a hotel. You will find that hotel restaurants, grills, and lounges are nearly always more expensive than neighborhood restaurants. It is worth wandering up and down the nearby streets to see if you can find something less expensive and more enjoyable. Even the hotel employees might suggest nearby restaurants. Coffee shops in a hotel (or airport) are less expensive than restaurants. Snack bars are even cheaper, but you may have to stand or sit at the counter.

Restaurants

Because the United States is home to so many different nationalities, one can find almost any kind of restaurant in the large cities. Listings in the classified telephone directory (Yellow Pages) may be by national cuisine or by area of the city or both. Restaurants range widely in price. Many post their menus in the window so you can get an idea of prices before you enter. If not, you may want to ask to see a menu before you are seated, or else just ask about the price range. Appearances from the outside can be deceptive—what looks small and inconspicuous may turn out to be very expensive, or a nicely decorated place may be quite moderate. It works both ways. You can get a good meal for about five dollars or slightly more if you eat in snack bars, fast-food chains, or drugstores, but in a medium-priced city restaurant you should expect to pay fifteen dollars and up per person—with wine or drinks extra. Prices in big cities go upward fast!

If you are going to a middle- or upper-level restaurant to dine, telephone ahead for a reservation—the earlier the better. Keep to the time of your reservation or else phone to say you will be late. Good restaurants will not hold reservations for more than a short time. If you are turned away or asked to wait because you have not reserved ahead, don't take it personally. The management has no choice. Fire laws are extremely strict about the number of occupants, and unannounced fire inspections are frequent. No restaurant owner dares overcrowd his or her establishment.

Quick and Cheap

Cafeterias, fast-food chains, coffee shops, lunch counters, and diners offer quick and inexpensive meals. The food and handling are inspected regularly by government officials, so you can usually feel safe about the food, although you are advised to choose a clean-looking place nonetheless. These places are crowded with people at normal mealtimes, particularly over the lunch hour, but if you eat a little early or a little late, you can usually get a seat without waiting too long. They can be found everywhere, are open long hours, and are useful in keeping your food budget down.

Diners are often found on the outskirts of towns. They vary from clean and shiny to rather old and run down. Truck drivers often stop at them because they are likely to have good parking facilities and serve large portions of good food at low prices. Furthermore, there is often an interesting cross section of people in them, especially in the early morning hours when the long-distance truck drivers are eating breakfast. You do not generally tip at snack bars or cafeterias where you serve yourself or at fast-food restaurants, but you do leave a minimum tip at lunch counters, say 10 percent.

Fast-food shops (where a limited menu is precooked and ready for rapid dispensing and quick consumption) have become very widespread and popular in the United States. Such chains as McDonald's, KFC, Burger King, and Pizza Hut cater to millions of people who want quick service and fairly good food in clean, simple surroundings. There is no tipping, though in many cases you are expected to clear your own table and discard your trash in the containers provided. Fast-food shops are especially appealing to children and young people.

Bars

Some American bars are loud, smoky, and crowded; others are rather dark and meant for quiet conversation. Some bars are now a common meeting place for singles and can be quite lively, with a dance floor and loud music. Some bars cater particularly to gays and lesbians.

Unless you name the brand of alcohol you want, you are likely to get a less expensive "house" brand, which for most people is perfectly acceptable. Don't order beer by the pint or half pint, as you would in some countries. Ask for a glass (usually eight to ten ounces) of draft or a bottle. There are many varieties of American beer and it is served very cold. Imported beers, ales and dark beer are gaining popularity. Japanese, Chinese and Mexican beer is often available in good restaurants and bars as well.

U.S. whiskey tends to be sweeter, more full-bodied, and cheaper than the whiskeys of Scotland or Ireland. Canadian whiskey is light. The main U.S. whiskeys are bourbon (made from corn) or a blend of several grains, known as "blended whiskey" and often incorrectly called "rye." If you want real rye whiskey, be sure the bartender understands. He or she will generally serve the blended type unless you make your desire clear.

If you like your drink at room temperature, be sure to say "No ice, please." Americans like most of their drinks ice cold.

Hours of Meals

It is possible to be served a meal at any hour—including all night—in most large cities, though you may have to look around a bit.

Some places offer Sunday "brunch" (or you might be invited to a brunch at someone's home). This is a combination of breakfast and lunch, served about 11:30 or noon for late Sunday sleepers. If you are outside a major city, it may be difficult to find a place that is open after 8:30 or 9:00 p.m., though lunch counters, diners, and fast-food shops usually stay open late.

In people's homes there is considerable variety as to eating times. The main meal is usually served in the evening, except perhaps on Sundays or holidays, when it may be eaten at noon. In cities people often eat dinner about 7:00 or 7:30 p.m. Outside the cities most people dine earlier, at 6:00 or 6:30 p.m., or sometimes even earlier. The hour for cocktail parties is usually 5:00 or 5:30 p.m.

Finding Out Where to Go

Most cities feature inexpensive paperback books, usually available in bookstores, covering their eating places, or you can check local magazines and newspapers for advertisements. Your colleagues at work or hotel personnel will be glad to offer suggestions, too.

American Food Habits

Generally speaking, American food is considered rather bland by those accustomed to hot or spicy cuisines. Salads are very popular and are served all year round. Many people in this country have become calorie-conscious and are trying to keep down their weight. This is evident in menus offering low calorie or "weight watchers" meals. Grocery stores now offer a huge array of low-fat, "light," or no-fat foods, from ice cream to soup to snack foods. "Diet" drinks (meaning without calories) such as ginger ale or cola are also popular. If you do not want low calorie items, read the labels carefully to avoid disappointing choices.

Waiters in restaurants tend to assume that everyone drinks coffee, especially at breakfast and after dinner, but you do not have to do so! Some people drink coffee or tea with their meal; others drink wine or just water. When dining out, you can ask for tea, milk, soda, beer, wine, or water if you prefer these to coffee. Restaurants cannot serve beer, wine, or liquor unless they are licensed to do so. Normally, when eating in a home, it is considered polite to take whatever is being served and not to ask for something different—unless the host gives you a choice or unless you want water.

The main course in American meals is usually meat, fowl, or fish, but rarely is more than one of these served at the same meal (except that seafood can be used as an appetizer—shrimp cocktail, pickled herring, oysters, for example).

Most Americans eat quickly during the day—that is, breakfast and lunch—unless it is a social, business, or family occasion. The evening meal, however, is usually leisurely and a family time. Racing through daytime meals is part of the fast pace described earlier. Lunch breaks at work are limited to a half hour or an hour. There is also another reason—others in public eating places are waiting for you to finish so they too can be served and get back to work on time. Each one hurries to make room for the next person.

There is a real difference in leisure and timing here between a meal that is "social," meaning shared and enjoyed, and one that is "just a meal."

The Language of Food

Meat

If you order steaks, roast beef, hamburgers, prime rib, and so on, the waiter may say, "How would you like it?" meaning whether you want your meat rare, medium, or well done. If you order it rare, the meat will be red inside; if medium, it will be pink; if well done, it will be completely cooked (and sometimes dry).

"Rare" is likely to be cooked just a little; "well done" to be very well cooked. If you prefer, you can indicate something in the middle by saying "medium rare" or "medium well."

Coffee

If you order coffee or tea, the waiter will sometimes ask, "Would you like cream?" If you would not, answer "Just black, please," meaning no cream or sugar. Sugar is generally already on the table, and often milk or cream is also, and the waiter brings the coffee black. Many people now ask for "decaf," meaning decaffeinated coffee.

Coffee is a popular American drink at all hours of the day. It varies enormously in quality; you will just have to experiment to find places that make it the way you like it. Espresso and other specialties are often available, but you have to ask for them.

Tea

Tea is much less popular in the United States than coffee. It is often quite tasteless; perhaps we make it poorly because we don't drink it as much as other nationalities do. In public places tea is usually a shock to the newcomer. A cup of hot water (no longer boiling if it ever was) is brought in with a tea bag in the saucer. You are supposed to put the bag into the water and leave it there until the tea is as strong as you like it. In private homes one will sometimes find it brewed. Herb teas have also become popular in the United States.

Other Drinks

Next after coffee, Americans are likely to drink Coke or other soft drinks, milk, or fruit juices. Iced tea is usually good and is very popular in summer, as is iced coffee. If you want to drink water, you may have to ask for it, except in the more expensive restaurants. It is safe anywhere.

Eggs

The waiter at a restaurant will ask you, "How do you want your eggs?" Your answer can include any one of a wide range of possibilities: boiled, fried, scrambled, or poached; with or without ham or bacon or sausage. You also indicate the number of eggs you want. Most Americans consider one or two eggs normal. Boiled eggs are emptied into a cup—rarely, if ever, eaten out of the shell. Fried eggs may be "sunny-side up," meaning fried on one side only (with the yellow face showing); "over," meaning well fried on both sides; or "over easy," meaning fried lightly on both sides.

The addition of one or two slices of bacon, ham, or sausage may be quite expensive. Take a look at the price on the menu before ordering. Usually a listed breakfast is less expensive than ordering side dishes.

French Fries and Coleslaw

French fries are fried potatoes—like British "chips." You often get them with a meal whether you order them or not. The same is true of coleslaw—sliced cabbage and mayonnaise. If these are served with the meal, there is no extra charge for them.

Hot Dogs and Hamburgers

Usually hot dogs are eaten in a long bread roll. The meat can be either beef or pork. You have your choice of adding tomato ketchup (spiced tomato sauce), mustard, pickle, relish, or onion (chopped and raw). Some people put all of these on at once! There is no charge for such condiments.

Hamburgers are one of the few purely American dishes. They are the staple of the fast-food chains (McDonald's, for example) and vary significantly in quality from restaurant to restaurant. They are supposed to be made of pure beef, with varying percentages of fat, though sometimes soybeans are mixed in with the meat. In both restaurants and fast-food places, unless you specify what you *don't* want, your burger usually comes with lettuce, tomato, onion, pickle, and a mayonnaise-type sauce.

13

Getting in Touch with People

Postal Service

The U.S. Postal Service is sometimes criticized by Americans for losing mail and for being slow, especially in the large cities, where millions of pieces are handled daily. Deliveries are made only once a day, and not on Sundays. There are often long lines at post offices, so it is a good idea to buy books of stamps or rolls of stamps to avoid frequent trips to the post office.

For ordinary mail within the United States, buy a supply of first-class stamps; for overseas, buy a supply of air-letter forms or lightweight stationery and appropriate stamps. If you have such supplies for your normal daily needs, you can then drop your letters into the nearest mailbox and avoid standing in long lines at the post office. Remember, though, to have your letter weighed if you suspect it is over the allotted weight. If you must go to the post office, try to avoid the lunch hour or the four to five o'clock rush when every mailing clerk in the city is bringing in the day's office mail.

In the United States, zip codes follow the name of the city and state; they do not precede the city as in Europe, South America, and other places.

Sending Money by Mail
If you want to send money abroad by mail, be sure to ask for an

international postal money order. You must clearly specify that you want an *international* form.

Types of Mail Service

Inside the United States, all first-class mail is shipped by air without extra cost. An airmail indication is not needed on the envelope. If you want to be sure an important letter has been received, send it registered or certified and ask for a return receipt. For extra cost, it is possible to use Priority Mail for special handling.

If you are interested in something besides the usual first-class postage, ask at the post office for special delivery or insured mail. Express mail, the fastest service, is delivered within twenty-four hours but, of course, costs a great deal more than other mail delivery. The post office is only one of a growing number of express delivery companies, and prices for an overnight letter vary.

Parcels

There are many rules and regulations governing the mailing of packages. Permissible sizes and weights vary. Tape is now used to secure parcels instead of string, which used to catch in the postal machines. You can buy it in stationery stores, most supermarkets, and some pharmacies. (The P.O. discourages paper nowadays.)

There are special rates for books and printed matter. Ask the postal clerk about them. If you are sending books overseas, ask about surface and air postage rates.

United Parcel Service (UPS), Federal Express, and other services are taking over much parcel delivery within the United States and overseas, being both cheaper and quicker in many cases. It is worth calling them for any large parcels (check the phone book). They will pick up parcels from your house or office, though, of course, they charge for doing so.

Telephones

The United States is totally dependent on telephones. Almost everyone uses the telephone to conduct business, to chat with friends, to make or break social engagements, to shop (catalogue companies are flooding the mail delivery system, encouraging the customer to phone in purchases by credit card), and to obtain all kinds of information. Telephones save your feet and endless amounts of time—not to mention multiple bus or subway fares. It is the chief means of communication in the United States. People are also increasingly relying on fax machines and e-mail to send information to another person or to a business.

Some visitors from other countries hesitate to telephone at first because they are afraid that they will be bothering the other person. Within normal hours—after 8:30 in the morning and before 9:00 at night—people are used to the telephone ringing and will not mind at all. Most offices have an employee whose job it is to answer the phone from 9 A.M. to 5 P.M. You need never worry about calling a business concern for information, nor will you find them closed at lunchtime, though of course a particular individual may be out.

It is simple and quick to have a phone installed. Just call the business office of the local telephone company (see the front of the local telephone directory). They will install it on a specific day by appointment, when it is convenient for you. You must be at home to tell them where you want it placed. Unfortunately, sometimes the process is much more expensive for students, who may have to make a large deposit to initiate service.

There are a number of companies which offer long-distance services. AT&T, MCI and Sprint are the three largest. If you have your own phone, you may want to ask for literature from all three companies so that you can compare their services and prices (see the telephone book for addresses). Telephone companies offer many services, so you can compare these services before you make a decision. All the phone companies have special reduced rates for in-state, domestic, and international calls. Some of these are very advantageous, particularly if you call the same number frequently.

You may rent or purchase your own telephone. If you rent a phone from the telephone company, color and fancy designs cost more. Most people purchase their own phone. Some phone companies require that you purchase your own equipment. There are a great many stores that offer a vast array of phones to buy. Second extensions may be useful in big or busy houses and are not expensive.

You will be charged a basic monthly rate by your local telephone company; calls outside the local calling area will be billed by the company you choose as your long-distance carrier. You can send telegrams and cables from your home telephone; these too will appear on your telephone bill at the end of the month.

When your telephone is installed, you will be given two directories—the regular directory, in which names of people with phones are listed alphabetically, and the Yellow Pages. In smaller cities, these are often in one book. It is worthwhile to sit down and really study these books when you first get them. They contain a great deal of information about using the telephone, special services that are available (including time, weather, or traffic information), rates, times of the week when one can phone most cheaply, area codes, state zip codes, and so on. The Yellow Pages lists all businesses, organizations, restaurants, stores, and services in your area in such a way that you can quickly find whatever you need. If you study that directory, you will learn much about your city and the range of what is available: schools; clubs; organizations; public swimming pools; all kinds of instruction and classes; where to buy special foods or spices; where to have repairs made on all sorts of goods; restaurants by nationality; and places where you can rent furniture, television sets, stereos, children's cribs, crutches, or a wide range of articles (look under "Rental Service").

The Yellow Pages, which is updated every year, can become one of your best friends if you take the trouble to get to know it well.

Telephone Credit Cards

As soon as you select your telephone company and have your own number, you can call the business office and ask for a credit card. This is free and is a great convenience, enabling you to make calls or send cables from any telephone, public or private, and have the call charged to your home account. This often saves you from having to struggle with exact change in a telephone booth, particularly for a long-distance call, and makes it possible to call from a friend's home or office without imposing on his or her generosity.

Public Telephones

Public telephones here are widespread. You will find them in bus and air terminals, railroad stations, stores, hotels, the lobbies of many office buildings, restaurants, gasoline stations, and in small booths along streets and highways. Instructions for use are found on each phone. Long-distance and overseas calls can also be made from public telephones, but you must have either a telephone credit card or a handful of change in nickels, dimes, and quarters. If you would like the recipient to pay the charges, ask the operator to make it a "collect" call or say you wish to reverse the charges. All operator services cost extra.

You can ask the operator what the charges will be for a three-minute call before you place it. If you ask her to do so, she will tell you when your three minutes are up. You can talk longer, but you must pay another charge.

Two Types of Long-Distance Calls

One can make calls either "person to person" or "station to station." Person-to-person calls are far more expensive, but you only pay charges from the time you actually begin speaking to the person you ask for, and there is no charge if the person is not there. If you are uncertain whether your party is available, particularly if you are calling from a long distance, this service is worthwhile. In station-to-station calls, you start to pay from the moment someone answers. This is the better method (it is much cheaper) if you think the person is likely to be available or if you merely want to leave a message.

Check your telephone directory for charges for long-distance calls. As in most countries, calls during business hours are more expensive than early-morning, evening, and late-night calls.

Answering Machines

Answering machines are now so popular that you will find your colleagues and friends upset if you don't have one on your private phone as well as your business phone. You will hear a message indicating that the person you called is not available and inviting you to leave a message at the "sound of the tone." This may seem to be a very impersonal practice, but it allows busy people to receive or deliver messages and return calls. Answering machines can be purchased from any store selling phones. Be aware, though, that with both message machines and phones, you generally get what you pay for, so avoid the least expensive sets.

Telegrams and Cables

The Western Union Company handles telegrams and cables in the United States and overseas. International cables are charged by the number of words, and there is also a surcharge (an extra fee), the amount depending on the country to which the cable is going. Within the United States you may send a telegram or a mailgram. Telegrams are delivered by telephone or to your home or business; mailgrams are sent to you by regular mail service.

You send cables and telegrams by telephoning Western Union or visiting a Western Union office. You can also send and receive money by cable.

14

Safety and Emergencies

Everyone knows that cities around the world are full of problems and sometimes dangerous; however, you need not miss the many advantages cities offer if you take precautions and use common sense. Then the chances of having a misfortune—while not totally removed—are very much diminished.

Safety on the Streets

When you walk after dark, keep to the more traveled and better-lit streets. If you have to go through dangerous areas, go by bus or taxi. Try to board your bus in a populated area rather than at a bus stop in a deserted locality.

Avoid parks after dark; if you are passing one, walk on the opposite side of the street. People with bad intent often loiter in dark places. They like the edges of parks because they can make a quick escape. They also like doorways and alleys. If you feel apprehensive, walk on the curb side of the sidewalk.

If you have to wait in a train or bus terminal at night, do so in the main waiting room, where it is light and people are passing, or else choose a place in sight of a guard or police officer. Avoid subway travel in the late evening when stations are likely to be fairly deserted.

Most—but not all—crime in the United States takes place in dark, rather predictable places where there are few people about. Reasonable precautions such as the above markedly reduce one's chance of trouble. Find out about neighborhoods or areas of the city to avoid after dark (or at any time).

Security at Home

Locks only work if you use them! Never leave the door to your house, hotel, or apartment unlocked; be careful not to leave a key in the door by mistake, even for a short time. Also, don't leave your door open, ajar, or unlocked, even if you are just going out to empty the trash or talk with a neighbor. It is a good precaution to use the inside chain on the door, especially at night. Most hotels, apartments, and homes are now equipped with dead-bolt locks in addition to the regular locks on the doorknobs.

Most city apartments have peepholes through which you can see who is at your door before you open it. Others have TV systems in the front lobby or some voice identification arrangement. Use whatever system is provided; it is there for your protection. If you live on the ground floor or facing a fire escape and are worried about your windows, talk to the superintendent about window locks or extra metal screens. Don't open a door unless you know who is there. Don't admit a salesperson, a repairman, or a deliveryperson unless you know them or are expecting them. Many service people carry an identification card issued to them by their companies. Ask to see it.

None of this is meant to frighten you, but it is common sense. If you use the various safeguards that exist, then you can feel secure, relaxed, and protected. If you do not, you are taking a chance almost anywhere nowadays.

Should you lock yourself out of your apartment by mistake, the superintendent can let you in again with a master key kept for such emergencies. Some people also leave a spare key with a trusted neighbor for just such moments of need. In most large cities there are locksmiths available on twenty-four-hour duty.

Look under "Locksmiths" in the Yellow Pages. They can be life-savers if, for example, you break off the key in your car lock after a party some night.

Fire and Other Emergencies

There are some simple precautions that will help prevent fires. Do not burn trash on your own. Most populated areas of the country have laws that forbid trash burning by individuals. Trash is placed in cans or strong plastic bags for pickup by the garbage collectors. In apartment houses, follow the trash instructions for the building.

Most fires are caused by burning fat, by defective electrical wiring, or by cigarettes. Never leave your home—even for a minute—while anything is cooking. The one exception to this rule is when you are using a slow cooker (such as a Crock-Pot), but read the directions for its use carefully.

All homes should have a small foam fire extinguisher near the stove; these are good for either fat or electrical fires. You can buy small portable ones at most hardware stores. Be sure to check the date before you buy—they deteriorate with age. Also, keep a box or two of baking soda handy. It quickly smothers grease or oil flames. Smoke alarms are required by law in most places. They are inexpensive, easily installed, and are good warnings, especially at night. They are also available in most hardware stores.

As mentioned on page 110, in most communities in the United States, the telephone number to call in case of an emergency is 911. In some communities it is a regular telephone number, usually listed in a prominent place in the local phone directory (such as the inside front cover). If this is the case, be sure to write the number down and post it on or near the phone. You should use the emergency number for fire, the police, and medical emergencies. You can also dial "0" to get an operator who will connect you to the emergency number.

Insurance

You might think this subject need not concern you. Unfortunately, there is a growing need for everyone to carry liability insurance as well as health insurance because an increasing number of people are claiming high damages after even the simplest and most ordinary of accidents. If someone trips on your front step, or your dog knocks over a child, or your cleaning woman gets burned on your stove, they could—and a growing number do—enter a lawsuit against you and claim damages out of all proportion to the accident. Courts assume that one is covered by insurance, and so they often award far more in damages than would seem reasonable to most of us. If you do *not* carry insurance for such a situation, you could be in serious financial trouble.

The term to use when inquiring is "comprehensive liability," which is included in a homeowner's policy. An insurance agent will advise you about the proper level of coverage for your income, the size of your family, and so on. Be sure to consult a responsible agent who will not sell you more insurance than you need. You should find an agent through your firm, someone you know in a bank, a friend, or a lawyer. When you get the agent's advice, it is a good idea to discuss what has been recommended with a colleague or friend before actually signing any contract. The more the agent tries to rush you, the more cautious you should be.

You should also seek advice on other kinds of insurance according to the value of your possessions and property. If you did not bring any jewelry, fine paintings, or furniture, you may not need to carry such property insurance as fire or theft, but you should discuss this carefully with a knowledgeable person. Insurance is expensive, and insurance agents may try to talk you into overinsuring goods that could be replaced without too much trouble if they were stolen. You almost never receive the full value from your insurance anyway. Often it works out to be a very small percentage of the value. The fine print on the contract is confusing but extremely important. Get someone who understands contracts to go over yours with you in detail.

Generally speaking, you need cover only a few selected, expensive, and irreplaceable possessions (such as jewels, furs, or cameras, for example) for theft. You will need adequate health and accident insurance because medical costs are so high here, and you need auto insurance if you plan to drive.

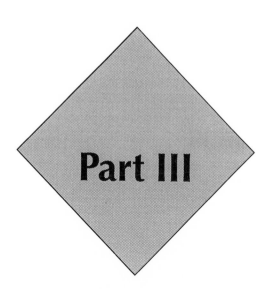

Part III

For Those Who Stay Longer

15

Housing

How to Begin Looking

As is generally true throughout the world, the farther you are from any urban center, the lower the rent will be. However, transportation may be so overcrowded and expensive that one has to balance these two factors in deciding where to settle. Naturally, it is easier to take part in the life of a city if one lives within its boundaries. For this reason single people and couples without children usually prefer to live as close to the city as possible. However, families with children are generally attracted to the suburbs, where they can find larger houses at lower rents, better schools, and a slower pace—not to mention grass and trees!

If your children are of school age, the quality of local schools should be of primary concern before you decide where to rent. Many families have found that in the end it was less costly to move to a fairly expensive suburb which had good public schools rather than to a less expensive neighborhood where inadequate or crowded public schools forced them to send their children to costly private schools. If there are several children in a family, this is a particularly important consideration.

Once the school question has been explored, commuting conditions should be investigated—train or bus schedules, highways, available types of transportation, commuting time.

Your employer should be able to give you helpful advice about schools and commuter schedules in suburban areas. You will be able to judge a good deal for yourself by driving through a number of neighborhoods. Talk to the local librarian or a salesperson or a gas station attendant; investigate neighborhoods or suburbs as thoroughly as possible before you actually select one.

If you are moving to a medium-sized (about 500,000 population) or small city (about 100,000 population) or to a small town, the housing situation will be quite different from that in large metropolitan areas. Neighborhoods within these cities may be as spacious as those in the suburbs, although houses will sometimes be older. Public transportation, however, is frequently limited in smaller cities.

Sources of Information

Your best source of information about either houses or apartments is likely to be the local newspaper. As a rule the week's most complete real estate section appears in the Sunday edition of city newspapers. Try to get a copy on Saturday! Usually the real estate section is printed early. Time is important as there is often tremendous competition for housing. You need to read the columns carefully the night before so that on Sunday morning you can telephone early (even at 8 A.M.) about rentals that seem interesting to you.

There are real estate agents in all localities, and some of them handle rentals. These can be helpful, but if you can find a house yourself through friends or the newspaper or by seeing a "For Rent" sign, it will be far cheaper. Agents charge steep fees—a month's rent is common, sometimes as high as 10 percent of the year's rent. Some companies pay such fees for their employees; others do not. Be certain you understand your company's policy regarding this matter, and inquire about fees before you sign with any real estate agency.

Reading the Real Estate Ads

Even Americans are confused by the terms used in real estate advertisements. A tiny hallway, an alcove off the kitchen, or an "L" in the living room may be called a "room." Sometimes kitchens and bathrooms are counted as rooms, and sometimes they are not. When you see "2-1/2 rooms" listed, you cannot be certain what this means. Neither can Americans! The only safe thing to do is to ask when you telephone: How many rooms are included in the apartment, and what size are they? Apartments are more expensive as you go higher in a building. You are paying for more light and less dirt and noise from the street and sometimes for a better view.

Renting a House

In addition to the rent, you will generally be expected to pay for gas, electricity, heat, and maybe water.

You also provide and/or pay for normal maintenance, such as grass cutting, window washing, leaf raking, and snow removal. If the house has a sidewalk, you may be responsible for having it cleared of snow within a few hours after each snowfall (usually within four daylight hours).

Furnished Apartments or Houses

The word "furnished" means different things to different people. You will normally be supplied with the essentials: stove, refrigerator, beds, chairs, sofa, tables, lamps. Minimal china and glass, flatware (often rather poor), basic kitchen supplies, curtains, and some pictures may be supplied. Sometimes, but very rarely, there is a small supply of bed, bath, and table linens and blankets.

You will need to supply your favorite kitchen utensils, some table linens or mats, extra lamps, coat hangers, whatever electrical appliances you want—such as toasters and irons—and generally also bath and bed linens and blankets. You certainly will want to bring enough of your own things to make you feel comfortable and at home. Your own pictures, books, decorations, and the like will make it seem more like home to you.

The word "unfurnished" means different things, but generally a stove and refrigerator are included—also towel racks, light fixtures, and other such built-in items often not included in other countries.

To Bring or Not to Bring

When you discover how expensive it is to ship household goods, you will probably agree that it often makes better sense to buy basic equipment, such as dishes, sheets, towels, and saucepans, here rather than to ship your own—unless, of course, your company is assuming all shipping costs.

Furthermore, you may want to think carefully about bringing any pieces you cherish, such as a delicate clock, an antique desk, your favorite chair. The best rule to follow is this: If the item were lost or broken, would you be sad?

Picture for yourself the crate being lifted by a ship's crane and then dropped into the ship's hold or sitting on a dock during a heavy rain. Probably neither of these things will happen to your things, since most goods today are packed well, but think about the possibility of such hazards. You may decide to leave at home your most valued possessions.

One more guideline: What will the climate be like in that part of the United States to which you are going? If you will be in sunny California, hot Arizona, or moist Florida, you should consider leaving heavy rugs, big upholstered chairs, velvet draperies, and the like at home. In hot areas it is practical to use rattan, glass, wicker, and so on and to use louvers or shutters rather than draperies at the windows.

Housing Agreements and Leases

Don't sign any agreement, normally called a "lease," until you have consulted a member of your company's personnel department, a lawyer, a real estate specialist at your bank, a well-recommended real estate agent, or an official at your university.

You should understand clearly *in advance* what the lease states about ending it or renewing it if you want to stay longer, provisions for damages, number of allowed occupants, rules about children or pets, rules that apply to subletting (i.e., renting to other parties while your own lease is in effect), painting or redecoration regulations, and hidden charges—sometimes extra ones suddenly appear for such items as a TV antenna or garbage removal. Also ask when the next rent increase will occur and what it is likely to be.

When you rent an apartment, you are normally asked for one month's "security deposit" in addition to the first and sometimes the last month's rent. The security deposit will be returned to you when you leave if there has been no major damage to the premises during your occupancy. The landlord or the landlord's agent will do the inspecting. This is not the last month's rent; it is an assurance to the landlord that any damage to the premises will be covered. For your own protection, you should examine the apartment carefully before you sign a lease and get the landlord's or agent's signed (written) acknowledgment of any cracks, stains, or other damages that existed before you became the tenant. Otherwise, you may be charged for preexisting damages two or three years later when you leave.

If you should be transferred before your lease runs out, you will have to negotiate with the landlord to terminate your lease unless this provision is already written into your original lease. You may have to pay the rent until another tenant can be found.

All such matters should be discussed in advance. Be sure to get professional advice before signing your name to anything. Once a contract is signed, it becomes binding. It cannot be canceled, and the terms cannot be changed without great legal difficulty. Furthermore, you will then have no opportunity for any further negotiations.

And so, to summarize, before you sign, find out the following:

1. Which services and utilities are or are not included in the rent—heat, electricity, gas, air conditioning, washing machine, etc.?

2. Do you have to pay a brokerage fee (if you found the apartment through an agent)? If so, how much will it be?

3. How often will the landlord repaint the apartment, and who will pay for it?

4. Exactly how long does the lease run? (They vary.)

5. What are the conditions under which you can end the lease if you should be transferred?

6. If you should want to sublet to someone else, can you? Under what conditions?

7. Does the landlord know the size of your family? Not all apartment houses allow children.

8. Does the landlord allow pets? Have *written* permission if you are going to keep a pet.

9. If you rent a house, who pays for lawn mowing, snow removal, etc.?

Utilities—Gas, Electricity, Heat, Air Conditioning, and Water

Stoves (often called ranges) are either gas or electric. Your heating costs may or may not be included in the rent—ask! If you have to pay, ask for the average monthly cost. Central heating systems generally burn oil or gas; in some cases, apartments or even houses may have electric heating. Be particularly careful about electric heating in climates with cold winters—you may find yourself paying six or seven hundred dollars a month, just for heat.

Modern apartment buildings are nearly always equipped with centrally operated air conditioning, which can be adjusted by the occupants of each apartment. If you live in an older house, it is likely to have window air conditioners. If there are no window units and the need is great, you can rent air conditioners on a monthly basis for the few hot months.

Most of the country operates on 110-120 volt current, 60 cycles, AC. A few older houses and areas are still wired for DC.

Unless your own small appliances can be converted for U.S. current, you are well advised to leave them at home. For small items, transformers can be a nuisance, although they work well for major appliances such as refrigerators or stoves. However, you can buy all kinds of appliances here at reasonable prices.

In most rented apartments there is no charge for water, but most houses are metered, in which case you pay either monthly or quarterly. Water rates are low.

You can drink water safely from taps anywhere in the United States. Do not drink from brooks, streams, or rivers, however. Pollution is widespread. Tap water may taste unpleasant because it contains a high percentage of minerals or purifying chemicals. If you find this distasteful, you can buy bottled water in the supermarket, have filters installed, or buy an inexpensive, hand-held filtering system.

Moving Your Belongings

If you are renting a furnished apartment or house, moving is a relatively simple matter. You move exactly as you would for a stay in a hotel, although you might bring a few extra items as indicated above.

If you are moving all your household goods to this country, you or your company will probably have arranged the transfer through a specialist. Large national and international movers have experienced packers and good equipment. You should inventory all your belongings carefully, making separate lists of (1) those items which are going into storage, (2) those being shipped to your new home, and (3) those going to be cared for in some other way.

Inventories should be reasonably detailed, but you can group together and record the number of boxes of kitchen utensils, children's clothing, desk contents, and so forth. You do not have to itemize down to the last spoon.

Before any packers come, you should sort out your belongings into separate categories as much as you can. Mark storage goods and those to be shipped with different-colored tags or stickers to avoid confusion or errors. You must also carefully supervise the movers as they work.

As the boxes are being packed for your new destination, mark each completed carton clearly in large letters on the outside as books, children's toys, kitchen supplies, and so on. This will help both the movers and you when you finally get into your new home.

When your belongings do arrive, you must be present to receive them. As the movers unpack, check to see that each item has arrived in good condition. The person in charge of the moving crew should make a written note of any damage before you sign the bill. Once you sign it, he will make no further changes. If some goods are damaged, immediately obtain a claim form from the moving company (or their insurance agent). Fill it out, make a photocopy for yourself, then return the original promptly. Time is important. Don't delay. Also inform your employer so that their transportation specialist can advise you. If you are not reimbursed within two or three weeks, let the transportation officer of your company follow up on your claim, or do it yourself. Don't let too much time go by.

Photocopies should always be made of whatever papers, letters, claims, or counterclaims pass between you and the movers and/or the insurance company. This is very important. If your company does not make the copies for you, take each paper to a public copying machine. You will find them in post offices, banks, stationers' shops, libraries, railroad stations, and even some stores! They are simple to operate and can cost up to a quarter per page. Having everything in detail and in the proper sequence in your files makes following up on any claim far easier and quicker.

Consult with your company some days before the movers are to arrive so that you know exactly what you can expect. Services vary widely according to the contract. Some will place your furniture, set up beds, and unpack china, silver, glassware, linens, and books. They are required to remove all packing debris. Some movers will connect your electrical appliances for you; most will not. Some will only set up large items and will not unpack small ones. Be sure to ask in advance.

It is not necessary to tip the moving crew, but most people do so in relation to the size and length of the job. Tips range from one dollar per person for a small job up to about ten dollars per person for a full day's job. It is also a good idea to have soft drinks and coffee available if possible. This is a tiring job. Be polite with the movers and try to stay out of their way. Time is money for them and also for you.

16

Shopping:
The Most for Your Money

One newcomer to the United States, when asked his first impression, replied: "So many things to buy." And so there are! You will find yourself being urged from every page of every newspaper and magazine and on every TV and radio station to buy all manner of goods which, in fact, you will be quite happy without. This constant barrage of advertising, with its emphasis on owning this or that in order to be happy, healthy, or more attractive, has given the United States the reputation of being very materialistic. It is true; this is an affluent and, therefore, materialistic nation. It is interesting to note, however, that as soon as any country grows in affluence, it tends to grow more and more materialistic. Traffic jams develop in country after country as more people are able to buy cars; salespeople work hard in most of the world to sell televisions, watches, furniture, food, clothes, computers, or washing machines.

Humans everywhere seem to be alike in this respect. As soon as there is any extra money, we seek to raise and *keep on raising* our standard of living. You need not be shocked at this, but you should look at the bigger picture: What do people do with their new prosperity? Does it enrich their relationships with other people? How creative are they? How hard do they work? How do they spend their money?

Because so much in the United States is mass-produced, there is a large quantity of relatively inexpensive goods available for everyone. You will find a tremendous range in price, based on quality, style, area of the country, and other factors. Comparative shopping is a good idea before you buy any major item. From all of the choices available, how are you, the new arrival, going to know what to buy and how to get your money's worth? In the first place, don't hurry. Take time to look over the various kinds of stores and examine the quality of their merchandise; read the ads carefully so that you can compare prices; touch, explore, and examine before you buy. In addition, some helpful guidelines are provided below.

Food

Supermarkets in the United States are always confusing. How can you decide what to buy amid an amazing choice of items?

Price
You can save a good deal of money if you watch for sales instead of buying only "brand-name" (a well-known company name) items at regular prices. Many supermarkets have their own label, and these items are almost always less expensive than brand-name items. You'll have to experiment because some brand-name items are indeed tastier or better quality than less well-known brands.

For example, one can of beans may cost $.87, another $.68. The more expensive one may be the brand that is most widely advertised and, therefore, best known. Perhaps you are only paying your share of the advertising costs. It is quite possible that if you buy the cheaper can, you will not be sacrificing quality, yet you will save several cents on just one small item.

Look to see if both cans contain the same number of ounces and look at the list of ingredients to see what percentage is water. By law actual ingredients must always be listed *in order of the amount contained.* Thus, if the ingredients read: "water, sweet peas, sugar, salt," put the can back on the shelf, for you know it contains more water than peas and that sugar and salt have been added.

Food Labels

The U.S. grading system for meat has nothing to do with nutrition, only with federal standards of quality for tenderness, juiciness, and flavor. The most common grades of meat are prime and choice.

Foods are marked using three categories: nutrition information per serving—calories, protein, carbohydrates, cholesterol, fat, and sodium; percentage of U.S. recommended daily allowances of these items plus vitamins and minerals; and the ingredients. It is important to know the size of a serving if you are interested in watching your weight or must eat carefully because of medical conditions such as diabetes or heart problems. Many products also have directions for preparation and suggestions for use.

Warnings

Although an increasing effort is being made to protect the buyer, there are still, unfortunately, a number of "shortcuts" or hidden factors that one needs to watch out for—sizes and weights, for example. A bottle that looks like a quart (or liter) does not necessarily contain that amount. In small print on the label, it may say "contains 24 fluid ounces" (a quart is 32 ounces). Packages meant to look like one pound may actually contain only 14 or 11 or 9 ounces worth of food. By law, weights must be printed on all food packages, under "net contents," so one can always look and see—but too many of us do not take the time and trouble. Often the print is very small—on purpose!

Don't be overly concerned about all these matters. You will gradually learn by experience and by trial and error, but you can shorten your learning time if you read labels and compare as you shop. You will soon find the foods your family likes and will learn which brands are best for you. Such care and study can save you a considerable amount on your food bills. The U.S. Department of Agriculture claims that those who watch carefully and who follow the weekly specials offered in all supermarkets can save in the neighborhood of 6 percent per week.

If you have clipped a discount coupon from the newspaper and you find the same item on sale in the store, you save even more. And some supermarkets offer "double coupon" savings, meaning you save twice the amount noted on the coupon.

Any large bookstore will have a selection of books that are helpful as guides to shopping.

Clothing and Fabrics

To judge the weave, quality, weight, and texture of cloth, a person has to feel it and decide for him- or herself. Labels are sewn into clothes to help you know the content of the fabric. There are also labels with directions for washing or cleaning the garment.

Suppose you buy a blouse advertised as a wrinkle-free blouse. How do you know what it is really made of? By law it must have a label attached telling the percentage of every kind of fiber used in the material.

Perhaps the label reads "cotton 30 percent, rayon 30 percent, polyester 40 percent"; perhaps it will say "100 percent polyester." Even if it contains only 8 percent polyester, it can still be advertised as a polyester blouse.

Many people never look at labels, but if you do, you will know what you are actually getting—which might make a difference as to whether or not you want to buy it at a given price, particularly if the label reads "dry clean only."

Returning Merchandise

If you have bought something and want to return it, you can do so with most items from nearly all department stores and often, but not always, from smaller shops. However, you must follow two rules: (1) the return must be made *within ten days* of purchase, and (2) you *must* have the sales slip with it. So do not throw away any receipts until you are sure you are satisfied with the item.

Sometimes during a sale, the store will post a notice warning customers that "all sales are final," which means that you may *not* return the item for exchange or for your money back.

If you are returning a gift that has been mailed to you from the store and therefore have no sales receipt, save the gift slip that accompanies the package and/or take off the delivery label from the front of the package. It has various markings on it that have meaning for the clerk. If you have no label, then ask to exchange for some item of equal worth. It is often easier to do this than to get a cash refund.

Warranties

When you buy new electrical appliances, radios, TVs, or other major items such as stoves, you will probably be given some papers with them. One of these is likely to be a written warranty. This means that if anything goes wrong, you can have the item repaired free of charge for a certain length of time—on some items as long as three to five years. You should read the warranty carefully. It probably asks you to send in a postcard to establish the date of purchase. If so, be sure to do it. In addition, write the date of purchase on the warranty itself, along with the serial number on your appliance. Keep it somewhere safe so you can find it if you need it. The warranty will be of help *only* if you have saved the papers and complied with the instructions.

Repairs

If you have problems with vacuum cleaners, toasters, radios, and so on, look under "Electric Appliances—Repairs" or "Radio (Vacuum Cleaner, etc.) Repair" in the Yellow Pages of the telephone book. Try to find a repair shop specializing in your particular brand name, if possible. Other kinds of repairs—china, glass, zippers, etc.—are also listed by item in most phone books. Repairs are very expensive, however, and you may be charged a minimum fee just to have the item examined, particularly if you ask someone to come to your home to repair a large piece of equipment or an appliance.

Telephone Sales

If anyone tries to sell you an item over the telephone, just say "No, thank you" and hang up without any further conversation. Credit cards, long-distance telephone services, magazines—all sorts of things—may be offered. Don't get involved! They may try to tempt you with every kind of prize, free demonstration, or gift. Most reputable firms do not use this technique for selling—any more than they use door-to-door salespeople—but newcomers to the United States should *take no chances* with telephone sales. It is foolhardy to do so.

Installment Plans

Generally speaking, avoid buying on the installment plan—paying part of the cost when you obtain a product or service and the rest in installments, most often monthly. Costs of carrying and amortization are also high and often hidden in the fine print. Once you have signed the agreement, you are obligated to make the payments. There is no way out, so tread carefully. Mortgages on real estate, financing on the purchase of a car, or similar loans on very large purchases may be necessary, but try to avoid burdening yourself with monthly payments on such luxury items as TVs, stereos, dishwashers, or tempting trips to sunny beaches in the Caribbean. You often pay one-third or one-half as much again as the regular price by the time all fees and interest have been figured. Buying by credit card and paying only part of your bill each month is essentially the same as installment buying. Although credit cards have the virtue of simplicity, you are running up extra charges if you don't pay off the complete balance monthly.

Buying Where It Costs Less

Americans do not usually bargain over prices, as people do in much of the world. What they do instead is shop around to find the store which offers the item and quality they want at the lowest price. Almost everything sold in the United States varies in price according to the store and often the time of year (just before Christmas is often highest; lowest is just after Christmas or during August, when many stores have sales). Sometimes the price varies according to state or local taxes. Many people cross state lines to buy liquor, cigarettes, or automobiles, for example, because there are wide fluctuations in taxes on such items from state to state.

Discount Stores

If it is important to you to save money, look for the discount stores in your city. They exist all across the country and are growing in popularity. Much of what they sell is comparable to goods sold elsewhere, but they can offer lower prices for any one or all of these reasons: there may be fewer salespeople, less service; usually there is no delivery service except for heavy items like refrigerators; floor space is often so fully used that the store is congested; the decor is simple so as to save the cost of fancy carpeting or expensive interiors; or goods may be sold only in bulk, i.e., in large containers or large quantities and stacked to the ceiling as in a warehouse. These discount stores may be appliance centers (Circuit City, for example); department stores (Marshall's and Ross Dress for Less, for example); huge hardware and home decorating and repair stores (Home Depot, Home Base, HQ, for example); office supply stores (Office Max, Staples, Office Depot, for example); and variety stores that sell almost everything (Wal-Mart, Kmart, Target, for example). In some of these stores you pay a membership fee (Price Club and Sam's Club, for example). Because they are so colorful and have such a variety of goods, these discount stores are often of interest to newcomers who find that wandering through them helps in learning American names for unfamiliar items.

In most discount houses you will find clothing hanging on long racks. Shoes, socks, or underwear may be piled up in bins. It is advisable to look for those which carry familiar brand names as much as possible, or ask a neighbor or friend to go with you. Although some of these are the very same ones that you would buy in other stores at higher prices, often they are made with inferior materials and poorly assembled.

Buying Secondhand

So many people are constantly on the move in the United States that it is easy to find secondhand household goods for sale. Buying secondhand is quite usual here. Many young couples furnish new homes this way. People who do not want to spend time shopping sometimes buy the entire contents of an apartment from someone who is moving to another part of the country.

If you look in the local newspaper, you will see advertisements in the classified section that read:

"Moving, entire contents of house for sale."

"Going to California; desk, large clock, child's bicycle for sale."

"Redecorating house, complete maple living room furniture for sale."

If you see something that interests you, call *at once* on the telephone; some things are often sold very quickly. If it is still available, go immediately to examine it. If you like an item, you can try bargaining. Then you must work out a means of getting your purchase (or purchases) to your house. This can be a major problem, but the easiest solution (if you have no friend with a pickup truck or van) is to look at ads in the local paper or in the Yellow Pages under "Trucking" or "Hauling" to find someone with a truck or to rent a truck or trailer (to attach to your car). Give a deposit to hold the goods and *get a receipt*. Don't pay the full price until you come back to pick up the item(s). Most people are honest but some are not—so you need to be careful.

Garage Sales and Yard Sales

Garage or yard sales are very popular events. People collect all the items they no longer need or want, such as furniture, glassware, china, clothing, books, toys, and so forth, and hold a one- or two-day sale in their garage or yard. Sometimes several families or even an entire neighborhood will hold a cooperative sale. Although many yard or garage sales are advertised in local newspapers, smaller sales may just be announced by signs on the streets near the sale site. Many people just drive around on Saturday mornings hunting for these sales. Good bargains can often be found, and talking with the owners and other customers is fun.

Buying in this way is a good deal more trouble than buying new equipment from a store and having it delivered, but it can also be much cheaper. Many times, you get real bargains and high quality, especially if the owners must move and are in a hurry to dispose of their goods, or if someone has died and an estate is being settled.

Thrift Shops

Thrift shops are run by charities (such as Goodwill or the Salvation Army) which first collect and then sell used clothes, sports equipment, books, china, glassware, furniture, and so on. The charities then donate the money they collect to some particular school, hospital, nursing home, or other institution.

There is no loss of face in buying at thrift shops. Many middle- or upper-class people donate to them, help to run them, and also buy from them. They are particularly good for such items as children's clothes (often outgrown before they were much used) or evening dresses, which the well-to-do donate after a few wearings, but which most of us wear so seldom that we want to buy at minimum cost. Many people go to thrift shops for ice skates, tennis rackets, or books or for pictures, lamps, or extras of that sort for their new homes. By law all clothing given to reputable shops has been washed or dry-cleaned and inspected.

A relatively new type of thrift store is the secondhand consignment store, usually specializing in women's (and sometimes children's) clothing, shoes, and accessories. The seller receives a percentage of the sale of her items—if they sell, that is.

Catalogue Sales

One of the fastest growing retail operations in the United States is selling by mail through catalogues. Catalogues will arrive in your mail on a regular basis, and you can purchase anything from gourmet food to fur coats by mail or phone. Growth in this sector has occurred for several reasons. People have less time for shopping—especially in two-career families—and retailers can reach a greater number of people. Most important is that shopping by mail is convenient, especially for the elderly or others who cannot move around easily. The disadvantage, of course, is that you cannot try on clothes or examine the product. Most of these services are very reputable and readily accept returns if you are not satisfied with the merchandise. Until you feel confident that the quality is good (you can check with neighbors or friends) and meets your needs, it is best to order very carefully. Don't be surprised to receive catalogues from companies you have never purchased from; many catalogue companies make extra money by renting their mailing list to other firms.

Shopping by Television

In recent years, a number of televisions shows—and even entire twenty-four-hour channels—have sprung up, aimed at the television viewer. These shows feature items at supposedly discounted prices, though you may frequently be able to find comparable prices in local stores. They display a variety of merchandise from clothing, jewelry, clocks, luggage, and toys to exercise equipment.

To order from one of these TV vendors, you select the item you want, phone in your order, paying by either credit card, money order, or check, and wait for your selection to be shipped to you.

A word of caution: Many people impulsively order items from these shows that they neither want nor need—and cannot afford. It is all too easy to get carried away by TV salespeople urging you to call in immediately to take advantage of this "limited-time" offer. Take care to avoid this situation. Also, quality varies tremendously among these products.

17

Household Help and Care of Young Children

Live-in, domestic help is prohibitively expensive nowadays for all but the wealthiest Americans. More common forms of domestic help are (1) cleaning women, who come in once or twice a week, or even every two weeks and (2) baby-sitters, who stay with children when the parents go out. Otherwise, precooked and packaged foods, microwave ovens, no-iron fabrics, dishwashers, and washing machines—all time- and labor-saving devices—take the place of household help.

Finding Household Cleaning Help

The best way to find someone to clean your house is by asking people you know. Start with your friends or your business acquaintances. This is a common request, and you need not feel embarrassed. Americans are accustomed to helping each other find domestic help, just as they are to recommending a doctor or dentist. People will ask their own domestic help if they have extra time, or if they know a relative or a friend who might be looking for work.

Alternatively, ask the manager or superintendent of your apartment house. Perhaps there is someone already working in the building who wants more work. Sometimes the clerks at local laundries, grocery stores, pharmacies, or the like can give you suggestions. If you are known to be a regular customer, such people are likely to recommend people carefully.

If you cannot find anyone by word of mouth, there are other methods, though these tend to be less satisfactory. You can use a maid service, for example, listed in the Yellow Pages. Such services are expensive; on the other hand, they look after troublesome details like Social Security payments, insurance, and so on. There are also companies that offer housecleaning services. They send a team of well-equipped people in to clean your house on a weekly, biweekly, or monthly schedule and to wash windows, clean rugs, and do similar heavy work at regular intervals—or once or twice a year, as you request. Housecleaning services are a growing industry in the United States and generally provide excellent services.

Another option is an employment agency, although it is likely to be expensive and is not a preferred way. There is no guarantee that the person will stay with you beyond the period covered by the usually high agency fee. Furthermore, you may have to interview many people. If you use this method, be *sure* to ask for references, both for the candidate and for the agency. Not every agency is dependable, either.

You can also advertise in the newspaper for a housecleaner. The difficulty with this method is that you know nothing about the people who may come to your house to be interviewed. If you do follow this method, check each reference very carefully before hiring, and don't try it unless your English is very good.

Finally, you can answer an advertisement. People who are looking for work frequently advertise their services. This way of finding help is particularly useful in smaller towns and rural areas where it is easier to find out about your potential employee. In larger towns and cities be sure to interview carefully and check references thoroughly. Some of the best prospects are found in foreign language papers.

Help for a Party

If you have a cleaning woman and find her efficient, you can ask if she would like to help you serve in the evening. These women are often willing to help out. Sometimes they have friends whom they recommend, or they may send their daughters. If you would rather have trained help, look under "Maid Service" in the Yellow Pages. You can hire waitresses, cooks, bartenders, or butlers by the hour.

If you live in a town with a college or university, call its employment bureau. Some colleges hold extracurricular training programs in household skills or bartending to help students in getting jobs. Other students just sign up for general help and can be hired by the hour. Some are excellent workers; others are sloppy and irresponsible. Try to interview before your party so you can judge for yourself, and ask for references.

Baby-Sitters

Only one person in five in the United States lives within fifty miles of his or her birthplace. Americans move around a great deal and often live far away from their parents. Because they have broken ties with their past at a young age, chosen their own occupations, established their own homes, and developed their own lifestyles, few American children grow up surrounded by grandparents, aunts, uncles, and cousins, as they do in most cultures. This, along with the fact that modern American families do not have servants, has made the baby-sitter a vital part of the American scene. A "sitter" is someone who is hired to care for children for a specific length of time—usually relatively short—while the parents are out for the evening attending a party or taking a class, for example. Sometimes the baby-sitter is also hired for longer periods, perhaps when the parents are away for a weekend. In such cases the sitter is likely to be a mature and motherly woman. For a short period, teenagers, college students, and others (of either sex) are commonly employed on an hourly basis.

From the point of view of convenience, the best sitters are often young people who live in your apartment building or close by in the neighborhood. This gives you a chance to meet the parents and interview the sitter. If an emergency occurs, young sitters can call upon their parents quickly for help. Another advantage is that you do not have to take them far to see them home at night or pay expensive taxi fares. Finally, young people living close by can usually fill in quite readily on short notice or for short periods of time.

In an apartment house you can ask the superintendent for permission to post a notice for a baby-sitter by the mailboxes. This is often the best way to find out if there is anyone in the building who is interested in baby-sitting. Retired people as well as students are often glad to earn a little money in this way.

An excellent source for baby-sitters is a nearby college or university. Students frequently want to earn extra money in their spare time. The best procedure is to go to the school before you need a sitter and ask if you can post an advertisement on bulletin boards or put an ad in the student-run newspaper. With any luck, you might find one or two students who come from your own country and speak your language.

The disadvantage of all students is that they are often busy in the evenings, they are gone during their holidays, and sometimes they bring along their friends. The advantage is that they are less expensive than anyone from an agency and, being young, are likely to be more fun for your children.

Again, if you like your cleaning woman, she herself may be willing to do some evening sitting or may know of someone who would like to earn a little extra money.

Other sources could be the bulletin board of the local YWCA or the Girl Scouts, who sometimes organize baby-sitting services. Some scout troops train older girls, who earn service credits in this way. They are a particularly good possibility if you want someone to remain indoors and play with the children. Since they are young themselves, you might not want to give them outside responsibility—for example, taking children through traffic.

As you make friends, don't hesitate to ask if their teenagers would like to baby-sit. Often they are delighted. Baby-sitting is a popular occupation for teenagers, especially girls, so do not be shy about asking them whether or not they are available. Most mothers try to line up three or four sitters whom they (and the children) get to know and like. In this way they have alternate numbers to call when their favorite baby-sitter is not available.

A young couple with children, struggling along on a tight budget—especially students—often work out an exchange agreement with another couple, sitting for each other's children a certain number of hours or evenings a week. The mothers exchange daytime hours as well, giving each other occasional or regular free afternoons for such things as shopping, working part-time, taking classes, going to the hairdresser, or visiting friends.

Rates vary widely by location and age—less money for teenagers than for mature women, for example. You pay more for daytime hours than the period after children are in bed—until midnight. After that, rates may go up again. You pay more, of course, if you have several children or if the job includes preparing a meal. Many sitters don't want to cook and you should not expect it.

If you have a small baby and want someone older and more experienced than a student, look under "Nurse Registries" or "Baby-Sitting Services" in the Yellow Pages. If you employ the same person regularly for even a few hours per month, you must pay Social Security taxes (see below) unless you get them through an agency. In that case the agency will do the paperwork for you.

Day-Care Centers

Many churches run day-care centers during the week. Parents need not be members of the church to enroll their children. Some list parishioners who like to baby-sit; some have set up group baby-sitting for certain afternoons during the week so that mothers can shop or attend to other necessities. Most churches also have nurseries and baby-sitting services on Sunday mornings so that parents can attend services. There is usually no charge—or only a nominal one—for this service.

Public or private day-care centers and neighborhood centers are another good resource in your community. They may be advertised in the local newspaper, but there is such a shortage of good day-care centers that frequently one must learn of them by asking neighbors and acquaintances. It may be necessary to put your child on a waiting list, so it is never too early to inquire. A note of warning: Never choose a day-care center or nursery school without checking it out carefully *and* obtaining references or personal recommendations from friends or colleagues.

Taxes on Household Employees

Household employees include workers such as cooks, cleaning people, baby-sitters, handymen, drivers, and gardeners. Under certain circumstances you are required to pay Social Security taxes for those employees on a percentage of the total wages paid. This amount may be matched by the employee, or you may pay the whole amount. You, the employer, are responsible for mailing the total amount of tax to your local Internal Revenue Service (IRS) office within thirty days after the end of each calendar quarter. Once you have paid your first tax, the IRS will send you a quarterly reminder. There is a penalty if you do not pay the tax on time. The amounts involved are not great, even when you pay the full tax yourself.

You should consult a tax preparer, such as a certified public accountant (CPA), to find out what your obligation is regarding these taxes. Also, you can telephone the nearest office of the IRS and ask for the proper instructions and forms for filing this tax. If your friends or neighbors employ household workers, you can ask them how they handle this matter.

18

Schools in the United States

Education is an important part of American life, and the wide variety of educational choices is sometimes difficult for visitors from other countries to understand. One-half of all the people in the country between the ages of eighteen and twenty-five are enrolled in either a college, university, or technical training institute. All boys and girls up to age sixteen are required to go to school.

Education here is intended for everyone. Schools are expected to meet the needs of every child, regardless of ability, and also the needs of society itself. This means that tax-supported public schools offer more than academic subjects. It surprises many people when they come here to find high schools offering such courses as typing, sewing, radio repair, computer programming, or driver training along with traditional academic subjects such as mathematics, history, and languages. Students choose from a large selection of courses, depending on state requirements, their interests, future goals, and level of ability. The underlying goal of American education is to develop every child to the utmost of his or her own abilities, and to give each one a sense of civic and community consciousness.

Because we have no national religion and because our population is so diverse, schools have traditionally played an important role in creating national unity and "Americanizing" the millions of immigrants who have poured into this country. Schools still play an important role in the community, especially in small towns.

The American approach to teaching may seem unfamiliar to many, not only because it is informal, but also because there is less emphasis on learning facts than is true in the systems of many other countries. Instead, Americans try to teach their children to think for themselves, to analyze, to explore, to develop their own intellectual and creative abilities. Students spend much time learning how to use resource materials, libraries, statistics, and computers. Americans believe that if children are taught to reason and to research well, they will be able to find whatever facts they need throughout the rest of their lives. Knowing how to solve problems is considered more important than the accumulation of facts, which often grow obsolete.

Computers are used in many classrooms, frequently starting in kindergarten. If your child does not know how to use computers, you can help him or her a great deal by providing computer lessons in advance, even while you are still in your own country. To find such classes after you arrive in the United States, consult the school or ask a local computer store where classes are given.

Naturally, when any family moves from one country to another, the question of schooling for their children is always an urgent one. Unless you are in a small town, within or near whatever community you live in there will be available to you a variety of schools: public, parochial, or private; day or boarding; coeducational or all-boy/all-girl; traditional or experimental.

A new and interesting trend is starting among many schools, particularly on the west coast, namely a shift to a year-long pattern rather than having long summer holidays. These long holidays were established back in the days when the country was primarily agricultural. Children were needed on the farms in the summer. Now, however, most of the country is basically urban (or suburban), most mothers are working and not at home, and some schools are seriously overcrowded.

The year-round schedule works like this: Class sessions are held for forty-five, sixty or ninety days, followed by a break of fifteen to forty-two days, year round. At any one time a third of the school's students and teachers are on vacation. This means that a school with 1,500 seats can then accommodate 2,000 pupils or more. According to the National Association for Year-Round Education, by the year 2000 over 4,000 schools with almost three million students will offer year-round programs.

Cities are struggling with the problems of overcrowded schools and no funds to build new ones. In Los Angeles, 42 percent of the students are enrolled in year-round programs. It is expected that many more will follow as the number of students increases. Interest is growing in other areas of the nation where the population is also expanding rapidly. Full-year programs are currently under way in at least some of the schools in most urban areas.

Public Schools

The great majority of American children attend public schools, that is, schools that are tax-supported and free. It is often confusing to people to find that there is no national standardized system for all fifty states. Each state has been free to develop its own model. These vary so widely in quality, facilities, disciplines, and academic standards that people often move in to (or out of) a state because of the quality of available schooling.

To make matters even more confusing, local school districts have considerable decision-making authority *within* each state framework. City, township, and district schools have their own curricula, boards, budgets, and standards, even though these must follow certain broad guidelines outlined by their states.

School support comes primarily from taxes at state and local levels, rather than from national funds. When the federal government does contribute to education, it does so primarily in the poorer states, where local funds are inadequate. National funds tend to be channeled for buildings, transportation, or other projects which do not affect the curriculum. As we have said, Americans jealously guard their independence from their own national government. If there is a chance that, as a result of accepting national funds, the government may be able to exert some kind of control, such funds are often turned down by community school boards (elected citizens). There have been heated arguments—even riots and demonstrations at the college level—when citizens have felt that the federal government was exerting too strong an influence on curriculum through support of scientific research programs, for example, or military training, or other specific projects. Since many of our ancestors and many of today's new citizens have come to this country for the express purpose of escaping too much government control, this feeling still runs deep.

In line with this emphasis on local control over education, there are no national examinations at either school or college level as there are, for example, in France or England or Japan. College Board examinations, which are taken across the country for entrance to colleges and universities, are administered by a private organization, not by the federal government, and no college is compelled to use them. Similarly, a private organization, the National Board of Medical Examiners, administers a licensing examination for physicians. The results of these tests are accepted by virtually every state, although each state has its own examination system. This practice is common among other professions as well.

This state and local independence results in substantial variation in the quality of public education, even from one town to the next. In our fast-growing cities, elementary and high schools are nearly all badly overcrowded. In recent years many have been troubled with violence, teacher strikes, and other problems. In suburban areas and small towns, public schools tend to be more settled, with adequate facilities, reasonable ratios between teachers and pupils, and good academic standards.

As a newcomer, you may raise questions and talk as freely as you like about schooling with any Americans you meet. Many people here are deeply concerned about education. They constantly discuss the subject among themselves, and they will be delighted to talk with you about it also. Much is good and much is bad in our current educational establishment. We are in the process of reevaluating and restructuring the whole educational system of this country in order to meet our current needs and the urgent needs of the coming twenty-first century, including many new pressures from our vast and rapidly changing population.

Private and Parochial Schools

An extensive network of private schools parallels the public school system. Some of these schools are closely associated with a church or religious denomination and are called parochial schools. Private schools receive no financial support from tax funds and are, with the exception of some parochial schools, expensive—some more so than others.

Why do people spend so much money, often to the point of major financial sacrifice, to send their children to private schools? The reasons vary.

1. Classes tend to be smaller with greater individual attention than in public schools. Some children need this kind of supportive individual instruction.

2. Most private schools are highly selective; through interviews, references, and examinations (at least for the upper levels), they seek students of quality. This means that they can usually maintain higher academic standards than the public schools, which have to accept students of all abilities.

3. Discipline is likely to be better and academic standards higher than in public schools, which are often overcrowded and understaffed.

4. Some parents living in crowded or academically disadvantaged areas feel they must send their children to private schools to prepare them for admission to college.

5. A few parents prefer to send their children to schools sponsored by their own religious denominations.

6. Some parents seek a more homogeneous student body than is found in the public schools.

Those interested in finding out about private schools can write ahead for preliminary advice from the Advisory Service on Private Schools and Colleges (18 E. 41st Street, New York, N.Y. 10017). There are also directories of private schools available in the reference rooms of most large libraries. If you write from abroad, be sure to enclose an international reply coupon to cover return postage. If you will be in the New York area, you are welcome to visit the office after you arrive in the United States, but you can also get much initial advice by mail.

In your letter include details about the kind of school in which you are interested, for example, a school in or near a certain city, strong on academic preparation with the emphasis on languages, or a small coeducational boarding school in the country for a shy fourteen-year-old.

Include an indication of your price range if possible, ask about scholarship possibilities, mention whether or not you prefer a church-affiliated school, indicate your preference for day or boarding, and specify how far away from your base city would be acceptable. Send along a copy of your child's school record—that is, a list of the courses taken with the grades received.

Each private school has its own admissions procedures; some of them are difficult to get into and some have long waiting lists. Once you know the names of some suitable schools, write for their catalogues. Then follow their instructions regarding application for enrollment.

Boarding schools exist mostly for children of high school age, though there are also a few for younger children. If you happen to settle near a boarding school, you may be able to enroll your child as a day student. Otherwise, these children live in school dormitories and attend classes on the school campus.

Nursery Schools

There is such variation in preschools and nursery schools that it is best to wait until you arrive to see what is available in your neighborhood. Private nursery schools are often expensive, but there are also informal play groups, church-affiliated nursery schools, morning programs at local YWCAs, or other less expensive possibilities in most communities.

Little children often attend these for only three to four hours, two or three days a week, but they start to learn about sharing, following instructions, and being part of a group. They also enjoy the companionship of other children their age, which is often hard to find in city living.

If you live in a housing area where there are many small children and an outdoor place to play, you probably will not need such an organized group. However, in impersonal apartment houses, children are sometimes lonely. In addition, parents coming from abroad like to give their children a little extra help in learning American ways and English before they start school, which can be a rough adjustment.

If you do not find a preschool that you like near your home, you may find that there are dance classes, art classes, gymnastics classes, swimming lessons, or other activities for little children through which you can bring your child into contact with playmates once or twice a week.

Large apartment units often provide day care or supervised play groups for little children during certain hours of the week. Mothers sometimes pool their resources and take turns with each other's children, partly to give themselves an occasional free afternoon and partly to give their children needed companionship.

Relationships between Parents and School

Most schools have organizations made up of both parents and teachers. They meet together regularly to discuss and confer on various matters pertaining to the school—curriculum, budgets, faculty, salaries, library facilities, or whatever it may be.

Parents often volunteer to help with classroom or after-school activities. They sometimes make costumes for plays, play the piano, bring snacks or cookies for a party, or assist a teacher on a class field trip. Some come at regular times, to tutor children in the classroom, under the teacher's supervision. Volunteering at your child's school is a good way to meet people in the area and to learn how the school functions.

In good schools a real effort is made to have the home and

the school work together for the child's well-being. You will generally find teachers eager to talk with you about any problems you may have concerning your child—although the larger the class, the less time (understandably) the teachers have. Where size permits, there are often parent conferences—scheduled appointments so that parents can meet privately with one or more of their child's teachers to discuss particular problems or progress. You will also be sent notices of meetings or programs to which you are invited. You may be invited to a "parents' day," where you follow a child's schedule through a full day of classes. This is enlightening and enjoyable for most parents.

Both mothers and fathers are expected to attend such meetings and to show their interest in the school and their children's education. School functions also provide a good way to meet your neighbors and to make friends in the community. Since Americans enjoy meeting people from other countries, you will probably find your national background a help rather than a handicap in getting acquainted. This is true even if you are having trouble with the language.

After-School or Extracurricular Activities

In addition to their academic work, children in the United States are offered a wide range of activities sponsored by the school during after-school hours. These activities, usually called extracurricular activities, are designed to help broaden children's skills and abilities and to give them a chance to practice leadership and assume responsibilities, to supplement school courses, and to provide additional stimuli. There is often a range of activities from which to choose, particularly at the junior high and high school level. Nature clubs, musical organizations, science clubs, art and drama groups, or language clubs are common, as is a wide selection of sports activities. Virtually every high school has a student-run newspaper, often with a photographic darkroom. Some extracurricular activities take place during the school day, but many are held after classes are over. Even though they are optional, they are considered a part of the American educational experience. Parents encourage their children to participate in those programs that best suit their own special talents and interests. Students learn a great deal during these activities, especially in terms of relationships, social and intellectual skills, and a well-trained body.

Both employers and college admissions officers in the United States carefully consider the extracurricular activities in which students have participated, both during their free time after school and also during the long holidays. These are indicators of a young person's leadership potential, enthusiasm, creativity, breadth of interest, vitality, and personality. These qualities are weighed, together with the student's or candidate's academic record, to assess intelligence, perseverance, and ability to use what he or she has learned.

The School Year

In most areas the school year begins in early September and ends somewhere near the middle or end of June. A few schools, generally at the high school level, also offer summer sessions. These are optional, but they give students a chance to make up work that they have missed or failed, take advance credits or extra courses they have not had time for in the school year, or just become familiar with a school before the new term starts. Summer sessions normally hold classes in the morning, then offer a range of sports, trips, and leisure activities in the afternoon.

If you arrive in the United States in the spring with a teenager who plans to enter a regular school session in September, you might want to consider enrolling him or her in summer courses to improve English language proficiency, to make friends, or to gain self-confidence.

Desegregation of Schools

Progress in providing equal access to educational opportunity for both black and white children in the United States has been made since the Supreme Court banned so-called "separate but equal" public schools in 1954, but it has been very slow, particularly in large cities, in both the South and the North. Now, however, "re-segregation" is occurring in a number of communities where white people are enrolling their children in private schools, leaving many public schools essentially black again.

Efforts have been made to try to assure that more or less equal numbers of black and white children attend school together, but because housing is also segregated to varying degrees, this has required elaborate systems of transporting children (both black and white) to schools which are often quite far from their homes. Parents of both groups often object strongly.

Those coming to the States may read and hear a good deal about the issue of "busing" in many parts of the country. It is an emotional subject. In some cases it has caused racial violence; in other communities the system has worked peacefully and well. Some urban areas, where the problems remain acute, are now trying a new method of combining (administratively) quadrants of their own cities with parts of neighboring suburbs, trying to create a more balanced mixture of children without the need for long bus trips.

Although progress has been slow and all kinds of delaying tactics are still often used by dissenters, most education experts consider that there have been heartening and substantial gains, even though incomplete and geographically spotty. Advances are evidenced by the fact that all minorities (African American, Asian American and Latino American) are going to colleges in far greater numbers—to better colleges, and to professional and graduate schools.

In the long run, of course, access to equal education is the only road to real job equality. Most major cities still have a long way to go at both elementary and secondary levels, and much remains to be done in desegregating both schools and housing.

Summer Camps and Jobs

Partly because of summer heat but mostly because we began as an agricultural nation, summer holidays are very long. Children and youth get restless if they have nothing to do, especially when they are living in cramped city apartments. As a result, there are thousands of different kinds of summer camps for children. They are run by many organizations such as the Boy Scouts, Girl Scouts, YMCA, YWCA, or churches. There are also many private camps which, although expensive, provide horseback riding, skilled instruction in various specialties, wilderness trips, and the like.

Older teenagers are more likely to seek summer jobs or go off with their own age groups on camping or other trips. Many go backpacking in the mountains of the West. Anyone living in a city apartment may want to encourage such summer prospects for their young people.

Many teenagers earn a portion of their college expenses by working during the summer at such jobs as deckhand, waiter, harvester, construction worker, camp counselor, mother's helper, gas station attendant, telephone operator, or messenger. American teenagers are not concerned with status. Being unskilled, they try to find jobs at whatever level they can, seeking not only money, but also experience. They learn work skills, responsibility, and the ability to take orders and to get along with a boss and new kinds of people. As they grow older and more competent, most teenagers get better jobs, probably still unskilled but more closely tied to their fields of interest—in hospitals, political headquarters, newspapers, schools, or wherever. Students from abroad should check carefully into visa regulations, however, if they also want to use the long holidays in this way. The dean or foreign student adviser at any school should be able to offer advice here, but the visa question should be raised in one's home country before leaving.

Colleges and Universities

Community colleges (also called junior colleges) offer two years of course work, after which students either receive a two-year (associate) degree or transfer to a four-year college or university. There are over three thousand four-year colleges and universities in the United States, about half of which are private rather than public, tax-supported institutions. Tuition at most private schools is higher than at state-supported schools. Many universities offer graduate studies in various fields and have professional schools such as medicine, law, and dentistry.

In many countries it is very difficult to get into a university because of very competitive entrance examinations but easy to graduate once you are admitted. In the United States, it is relatively easy to gain admission to some colleges or universities but often quite difficult to finish all course work successfully in order to graduate. Universities and colleges rated at the top academically are very competitive, but most high school graduates are able to find a local college or university that may not be so competitive.

19

Dating and Teenage Life

The affluence, independence, and social freedom of American youth are frightening to many visiting parents as they contemplate bringing young people into America's teenage world.

One of the most difficult things to accept is the fact that, to a large degree, youth in the States sets its own rules, regulations, and patterns—parents here have less to say than in most countries about their children's actions outside the home, especially after the magic age of sixteen (the age of a driver's license and often a car!). This independence is threatening to many parents from abroad, who react by forbidding their children to take part in American teenage activities, insisting instead that they come home directly from school and not go on evening "dates."

It is difficult for a young person to be so excluded because in the United States there are no alternatives. Most teenagers date in one way or another. This is the way the transition is made here from parent-dominated family life to marriage, and it covers a long period of time.

From eight or nine years of age to about twelve, children are still interested in members of their own sex, and they love to visit overnight in each other's houses. Children, especially girls, have "slumber parties" or "sleep overs." This merely means that they like to spend the night together in one of their houses under parental supervision. There is much giggling, whispering, possibly some candy making, pillow fighting, and so on. It is noisy but harmless and is part of the growing-up process. In the summer, some boys or girls may want to sleep outdoors in a tent or tree house or on a "camp out." To children of these ages, sleeping away from home marks the first stage of independence, and they like to be in groups.

The next stage is an interest in the opposite sex. Long before they are ready emotionally or financially to marry, teenagers start dating or "hanging out" together. Groups of young people gather in malls or eating places or at each other's houses. They listen to music, watch videos, drink beer and soft drinks, and may or may not move on to stronger alcoholic drinks and drugs. Premarital chastity is not considered the major virtue it once was, and by the time they graduate from high school, many teenagers are not virgins.

Even though birth control devices are readily available, large numbers of teenagers engage in unprotected sex—and the incidence of teenage pregnancy and sexually transmitted diseases has grown at an alarming rate. Large numbers of young women seek abortions (itself a highly volatile issue among politicians and citizen groups), but a growing percentage of pregnant teenagers are choosing to keep their babies and raise them alone or with help from their families. Many high schools now offer day-care services for these babies so that their mothers can finish high school. Teenage pregnancy is a grave concern for parents and for American society overall. Not all young people, however, are sexually active, and sex education and the fear of AIDS have made some difference in teens' sexual behavior.

It is interesting to note that youth generally sets, and also obeys, its own rules. These rules vary by locality and age group, but teenagers do set their own standards to a large degree. Some groups are quite strict within their own codes, others more relaxed. Fashions and fads (whatever is currently popular) vary by locality and to some extent also by economic level and social background. Fads come and go within a group, but everyone tends to shift at the same time, and anyone who does not is considered strange. The penalty for not conforming to the rules is likely to be loss of reputation, loss of popularity, or both.

At any large school students are likely to be able to choose from among various *kinds* of groups, ranging all the way from what the young call "preppy" (that is, conformist conservative) to "jocks" (sports-minded), "nerd," "artsy," "punk," or "grunge." These groups are often identified by strange dress and hair or other styles. Although strong conformity is usual *within* each group, a young person is free to choose which *kind* of group he or she prefers to join.

Although Americans are known for their individualism, they are also "joiners." They enjoy organizing and belonging to groups to pursue their personal interests. This group orientation is especially strong among teenagers, and parents often become worried if their child likes to be alone more than others, or if their child doesn't have many friends. However, the young person who prefers to read or play the violin or be alone is quite free to do so, and may, in fact, be given considerable silent respect by others for his or her independence.

The greatest parental worry is sure to be what group of friends their children become involved with, for peer pressure among some groups leads to alcohol or drug use. Drugs, especially the prevalent and inexpensive "crack" (an easily ingested form of cocaine) is disturbingly popular in the United States—at all ages, starting as young as eleven or twelve. Unfortunately, drugs are easy to obtain in or near virtually all schools, and students are under great pressure from their peers to try them. Many do, however, resist. In fact, there is at present a relatively strong counterreaction among both young people and adults to drug and alcohol use, and in reality, the number of people who become addicted to drugs is small relative to the size of the population.

Parents are advised to talk quite freely with school counselors and other parents about the situation in a given school—before enrollment if possible. Teachers and administrators are all deeply concerned too. Most will talk with you honestly about these issues if you ask them.

Many middle-class American youth are quite affluent. Some earn their spending money themselves. Teenagers often have cars, which is disturbing to some foreign visitors to whom an automobile is a luxury. In the United States, however, having a car is not necessarily considered luxurious living. Distances in this country are great, and public transportation is sometimes limited, especially outside major cities. Teenagers often need cars to get to jobs, attend classes, or meet their friends.

The majority of American young people are responsible, hardworking, and stable, despite the drug and alcohol problem and despite the fact that the contrary is regularly reported abroad. Unfortunately, those who are spoiled, irresponsible, apathetic, or disillusioned are sometimes more visible.

Many of the problems of youth result from the massive social changes that are being experienced in this country—not only drugs, but also high divorce rates, unemployment, insecurity, major shifts in population, and the breakdown of moral and sex codes.

The more one's children spend time with stable families, with people who are active in religious organizations or school or community affairs, or with people who have jobs, the less likely they will be to find themselves among disillusioned or irresponsible groups of young people. The more active they are in sports and other school activities, the more likely they are to be with other healthy-minded youth. The point is, though, that today parents cannot assume that all is well. They must be alert to what is going on in the school, in the neighborhood, and among their children's companions.

Despite worries over teenage morality in this open society, parents will find much that is good in the system, too. The depth and freedom of discussion, the vitality and initiative, a deep sense of public and community service among many, and the easy camaraderie of American youth can provide great experiences for young visitors. The newcomers will inevitably take part in life with their school friends. One should not try to prevent it. If they are made to seem "different" by parental decree, they may become very lonely, for they will be cut off from their schoolmates.

Parents can exert an indirect influence, however. First, of course, they have the all-important choice of neighborhood and school. In addition they can encourage, in an inconspicuous way, certain of their children's friendships more than others. They can provide outside activities with different young people—ski trips, for example, or volunteer projects, or a photography class, or summer excursions. Parents should get to know their child's school and other parents, join the parent-teacher group, attend all school functions, and offer their services on school committees. The more you take part in the school life, the more you will understand your child and his or her friends.

You should not come to America worried about your children. As we said above, the majority of American young people are serious-minded and responsible. Undeniably, however, in this troubled world, youth is restless everywhere, and problems do arise. Since American parents as well as visitors are naturally concerned about any difficulties their children may be experiencing, there are many sources of advice and guidance in this country, all of which are freely available to any parent. If you are concerned, you will be able to ask advice. Nearly all schools, for example, have counselors. It is the job of these men and women to advise either students or parents who are perplexed or experiencing difficulties in any way. It might be wise for you and your children to go together to talk with your school's counselor soon after your arrival, well before there are any problems. Ask the counselor about the local dating situation, the prevalence of drug and alcohol use, school activities, and areas of concern in both the community and the school. Then you can plan your choices instead of just finding your way by chance.

Most public libraries have "young adult" sections. Librarians will help you to find useful information if you ask their aid. As in every other phase of adjusting to this new culture, you should feel free to ask those around you for their ideas and advice. You will find other parents interested in your thoughts, your problems, and your reactions to youth issues in the United States. They will not be embarrassed to discuss the subject, and you need feel no hesitation either. Remember, though, that parents' roles in this country might be different from those in your country. Just as your children are learning to live in a new culture, you must also do the same. This doesn't mean a breakdown of the values you adhere to, but it does mean trying to understand other values that you see represented all around you.

20

Religion—In
and out of Church

In large cities it is possible to find places of worship for most of the major faiths, including Islam, Hindu, and Buddhism. This reflects again the variety of people from all over the world who now make their homes in the United States. However, rather understandably, in smaller towns or rural areas, you will in all probability find only Christian churches (of several denominations) and perhaps a Jewish synagogue.

Especially in small towns, churches are centers for much social and community life. Here you will find such activities as church suppers, dances, discussion groups, sports and social get-togethers, youth programs, and the like. Although you will probably not be given a personal invitation to these events, you will be welcome at any of them; they are held for the express purpose of including everyone in the life of the church. Church groups welcome you, regardless of your faith.

If you do not see a church of your own faith near your new home, turn to the Yellow Pages under "Churches." If you find a church you like and want to attend regularly, just introduce yourself to the minister. If you make the first move, the church community will welcome you, help you to meet people, and assist you in many ways to settle into the community.

Our churches offer so much in the way of social life that some people find it overwhelming. You need not take part any more than you want to. People may urge you, in the desire to make you feel welcome, but if you prefer to participate only in the worship services, do not feel that you are obligated to do more. It is a completely personal choice. Among the types of activities you will find most churches offer, in addition to the services, are nursery schools for little children, after-school programs for older children, lunches, discussion groups or voluntary work opportunities, outings, prayer or Bible groups, and women's groups.

Many churches hold "coffee hours" after Sunday morning service. These are informal and friendly, and everyone is welcome to follow the group into the social room for coffee and cake or doughnuts. No one waits to be invited. It is open to everyone, but everyone is then expected to talk to people, introducing themselves, whether or not they know anyone. Have some refreshments, talk with anybody you see there, and leave whenever you want. It is a pleasant, easy way to meet people of the neighborhood and community.

21

Finding Friends
and Having Fun

The Land of Leisure Time?

Since machines have speeded up work in homes as well as factories, both men and women have more free time than ever before in our history. Flextime (coming to and leaving work at staggered times, often to avoid traffic congestion) and the idea of a four-day workweek are spreading. Because Americans play hard and rather loudly, a visitor's first impression may be one of mass fun and games—of campers rolling down the highways, crowded beaches, packed baseball stadiums, endless television. In order to understand the true picture of how Americans use their leisure, however, one needs to look below this noisy surface.

It is true, of course, that much leisure time is used to play. It is a country of sports—hunting, fishing, swimming, sailing, playing tennis, and golfing are available at all prices to all levels of people. Americans by the millions love both to play and to watch team sports like baseball and football. They bowl, run or jog, ride bicycles, ski, or follow active sports of every kind. Also, by the millions, they watch television, take part in community orchestras, make their own films or recordings, go camping, travel, garden, cook, read books, and pursue many crafts and hobbies. Being part of a do-it-yourself country, people enjoy building their own shelves or boats, sewing their own clothes, or developing their own film; they do such things for fun as well as for economy.

This is a "self-improvement" country too. More than twenty-five million adults are enrolled in one kind of course or another, mostly on their own time, at their own expense.

Volunteering

In addition to the time spent on personal pursuits, Americans volunteer a tremendous amount of time for the varied needs of their communities. It has been said that if all the volunteers of the country withdrew, the nation would come to a halt. This would include hospitals, many schools, libraries, museums, playgrounds, community centers, welfare projects, clinics, and so on.

Why do so many Americans volunteer to work long, hard hours, often at dull and disagreeable work, without pay? What is their motive?

There are several answers. The concept of cooperating for mutual benefit, a sense of interlocking responsibility, and a willingness to work together are all deeply rooted in American history. The original pioneer settlers had to work together to survive. They had crossed dangerous seas and risked all they had in their struggle for political and religious freedom. They helped each other clear land, build homes, and harvest their crops. Americans have traditionally valued their freedom and independence, and they still do. Deep-seated distrust of central government still remains in all aspects of American life. People still prefer to do things themselves within their communities rather than give a government agency control or wait for its bureaucratic delays.

Sometimes Americans volunteer because they want to achieve something for which no money is paid. So they come together to contribute their energies—as is also done elsewhere. They may work together to put a new roof on a church, to send parcels to flood victims, to provide summer holidays for underprivileged children, to build a new playground, or to clean up a polluted stream. People will give time after a long, hard day to work on a town zoning commission or school board or planning committee. They care about their towns.

Hundreds of thousands of so-called leisure hours go into hard, sustained, unpaid work on one or another community need. As you read the local newspapers, you will see that Americans are constantly forming new kinds of citizens' groups for some of the following reasons: to improve the lot of migrant workers, to take action against some form of discrimination, to fight crime, to elect an official, to protect consumers from fraud, to fight against drugs or drunk driving, or to do away with a pesticide that is killing wildlife.

One does not need to be a citizen to join in such activities. Once you settle into a community (even a big city), you will soon be aware of the varieties of volunteer projects that are going on around you. Anyone who is interested in sharing this side of American life will greatly deepen his or her understanding of the country. You can start by calling a volunteer center or contacting a local church, YMCA, or similar organization. Asking neighbors about what is available often elicits a helpful response. Or if you read about something that interests you in the local paper, contact the organization and offer your time or help. Most people welcome assistance if they do not have to pay for it. This kind of volunteering may open interesting doors to you as well.

Do You Already Belong?

Perhaps in your home country you already belong to some group such as Rotary International, Lions, YWCA, an association of university women, or a professional group (of journalists, chemical engineers, doctors, and so on). Perhaps you belong to a sports club—ski, tennis, soccer, or hiking. Many overseas universities have alumni chapters scattered around the United States.

If you are already a member of any such organization at home, look for its affiliate here and let them know of your desire to participate. You will get an immediate welcome. If you are interested in (but not yet affiliated with) any such group, try to become a member before leaving your own country. You will then automatically be eligible to join activities with your American counterparts on arrival without waiting for membership formalities. Such channels for making new friends will be most useful when you first arrive, so it is good to come with introductions and with memberships already established, if you can.

Interest Groups

There are, of course, many sports and activities which anyone can engage in without joining formal organizations. Hunting and fishing enthusiasts can find colleagues here in great numbers, as can climbers, hikers, skiers, bridge players, photographers, chess enthusiasts, bird-watchers, or cello players! Whatever your nationality, you can also find a national group in any large city. Ask at your nearest consulate or look under "Associations" in the Yellow Pages to find the Turkish Society, India House, African Center, or whatever exists locally.

Have You Always Wanted to Study?

Perhaps for a while when you first come to the States, you will want to study English or join an English conversation group in order to gain confidence in speaking. Or perhaps you will have time to acquire some new skills or to take a short course that has always interested you.

One secretary at the United Nations took a stenography course in her free evenings. By the time she returned home to Malaysia she was able to command twice her previous salary by expert reporting of meetings and conferences. Later she opened a small stenography school in her own country and again more than doubled her salary.

Adult education is widespread. Classes are offered in a wide range of subjects: painting, cooking, photography, languages, astronomy, computer programming. One need not necessarily have any particular qualifications to enroll in classes. Alternatively, you may be interested in taking more substantive courses leading to degrees, certificates, or diplomas. Just a few possibilities of subject areas are journalism, interior decorating, fashion design, business administration, accounting, and so on.

Both formal and informal classes are advertised in local newspapers. Look under "Schools" in the Yellow Pages. YMCAs and YWCAs offer a wide range of classes; the public school systems of most cities sponsor adult evening classes, as do community colleges. Ask for a catalogue of adult courses from the local board of education.

In addition, if you are near any of the nation's 1,800 colleges and universities, you will find they make courses, concerts, and lectures available to the nearby community. Usually these are held in the evening. You can ask to be put on their mailing list for advance notices.

Lectures

Many Americans attend lectures. If you like to be intellectually stimulated but do not have time for a complete course, you can follow any line of interest on a more casual basis—often free. You may want to explore new fields like oceanography, city planning, or outer space.

In addition to lectures given at colleges and universities, you will find that botanical gardens, civil rights organizations, government and political groups, churches, and museums also offer a great number of lectures, debates, and forums; so do international organizations, business groups, and professional organizations.

Get yourself on mailing lists (usually free for the asking), listen to local radio announcements, or ask your friends' advice. Easiest of all—just read the newspapers.

Museums

If your idea of a museum is a dusty row of glass cases or rooms full of badly lit oil paintings, try going to some of the museums in U.S. cities and towns. The art of display itself has become highly developed in this country, so that museums have come alive in recent years to an extraordinary degree.

In addition to many fine art museums, look also for natural history or science museums. Children's museums are sprouting up all over the country and usually offer a wide range of fascinating, "hands-on" exhibits. Photographic exhibits are often a particularly good way to understand the social concerns of a country. Don't miss the many small museums of contemporary crafts, African American history, Native American history, musical instruments, or coins. While at the museum one can often join a group tour or rent a small tape-recorded guide which adds much to one's understanding (rental fees are generally modest for two or three hours' use). Sometimes they are available in several languages. Those going to Boston, New York, Philadelphia, Washington, D.C., Atlanta, Chicago, Denver, Los Angeles, or San Francisco should plan to spend considerable time at the particularly fine museums in these cities.

Places like Williamsburg, Virginia, Dearborn, Michigan, and Sturbridge Village, Massachusetts, are whole villages, reconstructed as living museums to depict the life of our early settlers. At most times of the year there are live demonstrations of many old crafts, such as candle making, quilting, or the shoeing of horses. There are waterfront museums at Mystic, Connecticut, and the seaports of New York and Baltimore, where one may have the opportunity to board old sailing vessels. The old Spanish missions in California trace the history of Spanish settlements in the southwestern United States. Smaller cities almost always have some sort of museum depicting the history of the area; Palm Springs, California, for example, has the Desert Museum.

The Performing Arts

The United States abounds in theater, music, and dance, both professional and amateur. Most large cities have their own symphony orchestras; there is a wealth of experimental music and drama being produced across the country in college theaters, community centers, and small neighborhood theaters. Traditional theater and music are also plentiful. Movies, of course, are very popular in the United States, and there are many film festivals.

Theater

Ticket prices for theater in the big cities have risen considerably. However, you can avoid high prices by going to smaller theaters which often have excellent performances of the same plays, but at lower prices. Many cities now subsidize a civic center, keeping prices at a reasonable level. Ask New Yorkers about "twofers"—meaning two tickets for the price of one. Sometimes at the end of a long and successful Broadway run, or when promoters are trying to fill a faltering house, these become available. Often you can use them to see excellent productions at half price.

Theater tickets (and opera and concert tickets as well) are often hard to come by—partly because the urban population is rapidly growing, and partly because public taste is growing more arts-minded. There are various ways to obtain tickets—besides the usual one of going to the box office weeks in advance.

Read the theater reviews in local newspapers, and look for applications for ticket orders. Then write in quickly for tickets, sending a check or money order with your request. This is the best way if you have lots of time, but be sure to send a *self-addressed and stamped* envelope or you will get no answer. If you can offer two or three alternate dates, your chance of getting one of them is far better than if you specify only one (sometimes all the tickets in the house are taken over on a given night by a charity or special group). You can also order tickets by telephoning and giving a credit card number.

If theater is important to you, you can join a theater club in many cities and get tickets through them. They usually open their membership in September. Watch the theater section of the newspapers for advertisements. They send members reviews of plays before they open, as well as giving them the chance to buy tickets by mail in advance at reduced rates or season tickets for all the year's productions.

Discount tickets and theater vouchers are also available through various organizations in many cities. Ask your colleagues and read the "Arts and Leisure" or "Living" section of your local newspaper. In addition, many cities sponsor free performances of many kinds in parks, schools, libraries, and other centers.

Music

In New York and some other large cities, almost the only way to obtain tickets to performances of the major opera companies and concert orchestras is to buy season tickets. Inquire early in the summer for the coming winter season, if you can. After renewals are offered to old subscribers in June, then series tickets go on public sale. As season tickets are apt to be expensive, several people often join together to buy one series. They then divide the tickets among themselves, each going once or twice a month. This is perfectly legitimate and often done.

Another method of securing tickets for a particular performance is through ticket brokers. You pay (legally) a bit more per ticket. These brokers handle about 5 percent of all theater and concert tickets sold in a big city like New York. You will find brokers in the Yellow Pages under "Theater Brokers" or "Theater Tickets." You will also find them at desks in the lobbies of most good hotels and clustered around the theater district.

Dance

Modern dance and the jazz dance form originated in the United States and are vibrant American art forms today. Classical and modern ballet is also popular. Much of America's hopes, fears, ideals, tensions, and culture are clearly visible through its dance. Those coming from abroad can learn a great deal about the country by watching or by participating in dance classes, which exist almost everywhere.

Sports

Newcomers to the United States often find it difficult to participate in the particular sports they enjoy. Actually, it need not be so. Almost all sports are available everywhere, even in a crowded city such as New York. One of the first places to investigate if you are interested in swimming, tennis, badminton, gym classes, modern dance, or anything of an indoor sport nature is the nearest YMCA or YWCA. Most of these are well equipped and provide excellent facilities for reasonable fees. There are fancier and more expensive facilities for all such sports as well, often at clubs or hotels. Also, don't forget that any good bookstore has books on virtually every kind of sporting or recreational (including travel) activity by locality. Some colleges and universities also sell memberships to their indoor sports facilities, which are often of excellent quality.

Swimming

A great many swimming pools are open to the public. In addition to those run by the YWCA or YMCA, others are operated by the cities or towns themselves or by hotels or by swimming schools. When weather permits, there are often public pools and beaches available within a reasonable distance. Usually these can be reached by public transport—either bus or train—as well as by private car. Look in the Yellow Pages under "Swimming" or "Sports."

Other Sports

Read the newspapers or look in the telephone book under the name of whatever sport interests you: ski clubs; walking clubs; fencing, gymnastics, judo, karate, and aerobics classes; ice skating; squash and racquetball clubs; bicycle clubs; bowling clubs; riding groups; and bird-watching clubs. Golf and tennis are very popular. In addition to private clubs, nearly all cities maintain numerous tennis courts and golf courses which are open to the public for a fee. Ask your local Department of Parks and Recreation for booklets describing its sports facilities or visit the Chamber of Commerce or the Visitors Center.

Those who like baseball need only drift around the parks. Many games will be going on. Employees often form softball or baseball teams connected with different departments and have a full schedule of games. Usually they need, and welcome, additional players. Roller-skating, Frisbee throwing, and kite flying are all popular, especially in parks; one can also find paths for biking, jogging, or walking in these areas. However, it is not wise to visit parks after dark. They are not safe at that time in most places.

Camping and Hiking

Within relatively easy access, you will find excellent camping facilities in both state and national parks as well as private facilities.

You can get free booklets and maps describing public camping facilities and park areas by writing to both the individual state parks department and the National Park Service in Washington, D.C. When you write, state your specific interests. Information centers along major highways or in towns also offer booklets or maps of both public and private camping and recreational vehicle facilities.

All over the United States, there are thousands of miles of walking trails, all kinds of lodges and huts for hikers, and a great many campsites where you can pitch tents and find water, but you need to know where to find them in order to avoid over-crowded highways and too many people. You need to make reservations months ahead in these public areas; one of the disadvantages of our vast size and population is that we must often "schedule" solitude in public places.

Fishing and Hunting

The state and national booklets mentioned above also include information on fishing and hunting. You can always find fellow enthusiasts in your own locality. Talk to your colleagues, read the sports columns in the newspapers, or chat with salespeople in the sporting goods stores. Through such contacts you can find out what clubs there are in the vicinity and then ask about the possibility of joining one. Public-owned facilities are likely to be crowded; joining a group or club gives you access to more private waters and woods. Most clubs have reasonably open membership rules and would welcome your inquiry. They range in price from moderate to high; the lower the price, the more welcoming they are in general, but also, of course, the more crowded. The expensive clubs are, of course, likely to be the most exclusive.

If you are a deep-sea fishing enthusiast, there are boats and captains ready to take you out at almost any marina or port. Prices per day are high, but if you form a group and go together, you can divide the cost among many of you.

Birds

Those interested in birds should look up the nearest Audubon Society in the telephone book and ask about groups, activities, or sanctuaries in the area. The local library is another good source of information.

Watching Americans at Work

There are many people who do not want to become deeply involved in American activities but who are still interested in learning about the country. If you are among this group, you are welcome to take tours of workplaces. It is easy to watch a nation work when you visit people at their jobs.

If you cannot find out about possibilities through your friends, just call the place of business that most interests you (factory, bank, police training school, or whatever), and ask for the public relations department. They will be able to tell you whether they have tours (some factories schedule them regularly) or whether you can visit on your own. Tell them where you are from and why you are interested. In most cases you will find that people are friendly and pleased to have you visit as their guest, although they may first check with your office to make sure you are who you say you are. Your local Chamber of Commerce and city information center are also good sources.

Unfortunately, in recent years, we have become a little cautious about unexpected strangers, so be sure to make arrangements in advance. This way people know you are coming and you can know that your visit will be convenient for them. Then, *be on time.* If you must be late, be sure to telephone. They are doing you a favor by letting you come to visit their operation; don't take them or their time for granted. You generally do not tip or pay any fee (except for factories that have become tourist attractions), but a thank-you letter afterward would be much appreciated.

You can visit most kinds of factories and watch men and women working at heavy industry, precision manufacturing, or food processing. You can call on various kinds of schools, watch courts in progress, listen to hearings before government committees, and attend town meetings or meetings of school boards. Rarely are any of these private. Usually the public is admitted, although sometimes only by previous arrangement. Often there are tours for the public "behind the scenes" in such places as department stores, post offices, or newspaper plants. Again, contact the local Chamber of Commerce.

In this country you should not be shy or retiring. A little effort on your part will provide you with a great deal of insight into the American way of life. We welcome guests, we are flattered to have people interested in what we are doing, and we are proud to show them what we have.

Appendices

What You Can
Bring through Customs

You may be asking yourself, "What can I bring into the United States without paying duty?" "Can I bring gifts?" "Must I declare *everything*?" "Is there anything that I may not bring?"

You should obtain from the nearest U.S. consulate a copy of the pamphlet *Customs Hints for Visitors (Nonresidents)*, which gives full answers to all such questions. Below are *summaries* of the regulations.

Not Allowed

Some items that may *not* be brought into the United States without special permits are listed below.

1. *Drugs.* If you must bring in a special prescription, be *sure* to get a permit in advance. Inquire at a U.S. consulate for details.

2. *Plants.* No fruits, vegetables, plants, seeds, cuttings, or plant products may be imported without writing ahead for permission from

> Import and Permit Section
> Plant Quarantine Division
> 209 River Street
> Hoboken, NJ 07030

The reason for this regulation is that the United States is attempting to prevent insects or plant diseases from being brought into the country.

3. *Meats and hides.* To avoid importing animal diseases, permission is needed to bring in meats (including sausages, salamis, and so forth) and untanned furs or hides. If you wish to bring either of these to the United States, write to

> Animal Health Division
> U.S. Agricultural Research Service
> Hyattsville, MD 20782

4. *Goods from certain countries.* One cannot import goods of any kind originating in certain countries. Inquiries should be made to

> Foreign Assets Control
> Department of the Treasury
> Washington, DC 20220

5. *Gold.* There are tight restrictions regarding gold, gold coins, gold-coin jewelry or medals.

6. *Firearms and ammunition.* Guns and ammunition for sporting purposes only may be imported with permission from

> Firearms Division
> Internal Revenue Service
> Washington, DC 20224

No ammunition, pistols, or revolvers may be shipped in the U.S. mail.

Pets

Cats, dogs, birds, and so on, must meet certain requirements before they may enter. Ask at the nearest U.S. consulate for the booklet *So You Want to Import a Pet,* or write

> Center for Disease Control
> Division of Quarantine, M.S. E03
> Atlanta, GA 30333
> (404) 639-8107

Questions

If you have questions on customs regulations that cannot be answered by your nearest U.S. embassy or consulate, write

> Bureau of Customs
> Department of the Treasury
> Washington, DC 20226

Household Helps

Fahrenheit and Celsius

To change Fahrenheit into Celsius subtract 32 and multiply by $\frac{5}{9}$: $(F-32)\ \frac{5}{9} = C$.

Here are some examples.

Fahrenheit	Celsius
0°	-18°
32°	0°
50°	10°
68°	20° (room temp.)
86°	30°
104°	40°
212°	100° (boiling)
98.6°	37° (body temperature)

Metrics and American Measures

Except in certain situations (for example, measuring distance in races and in scientific fields), the United States has made very slow progress switching over to the metric system. You may, therefore, need some help in adjusting to our system of measures.

mile	a little over two kilometers; multiply kilometers by .6 to get miles
yard	just short of a meter, a meter is 11/10 of a yard; one meter is 3.2 feet (a yard is 3 feet)
foot	30.4 centimeters; 3 feet equals one yard
inch	about 3 centimeters (a centimeter is 3/10 of an inch); one U.S. foot is 12 inches
quart	almost the size of a liter (the liter is 11/10 of a quart); gasoline is sold by the gallon, which is four quarts
pint	a half liter (2 pints equals 1 quart)
pound	approximately one-half kilogram; a kilogram is actually 2.2 pounds
ounce	approximately 30 grams; there are 16 ounces in a pound; for measures smaller than an ounce, Americans divide the ounce: 1/2 ounce, 1/4 ounce, and so forth.

Clothing Sizes

Throughout the world there is an attempt to standardize sizes. However, there is still so much variation that shopping is always difficult when one first moves to another country.

Even with a size-conversion chart, you would do well to shop with your tape measure in hand and, above all, try clothing on. Body shapes, fullness, armholes, proportion of body size to neck band or sleeve length vary according to national origin. If your size is not "standard" by American measures, you may have to search a bit among unfamiliar terms such as "junior," "petite," "plus" (women) and "big and tall" (men). Large department stores often have what they call "Personal Shopping Departments" or "Service Desks" where you can get help if you ask for it. Many major stores in large cities have salespeople who can speak a number of languages.

The following comparison of American with European sizes may be helpful to Asians, Africans, or South Americans as well, since many countries follow either British or continental measurements. Please realize, however, that there is considerable variation from country to country and even within countries as well. The information below, therefore, is included only as a guide and is not to be taken necessarily as an exact measure.

Women

Suits, Dresses, and Coats

U.S.A.	8	10	12	14	16	18	20
British	10	12	14	16	18	20	22
or	(34)	(36)	(38)	(40)	(42)	(44)	
Continental	38	40	42	44	46	48	

Sweaters, T-shirts, and Other Tops

Small	Sizes under 10
Medium	Sizes 10-12
Large	Sizes 14-16
Extra Large	Sizes 18-20

In skirts, dresses, and coats, half sizes are usually intended for the short-waisted, stocky figure.

Stockings

U.S.A.	8	$8\frac{1}{2}$	9	$9\frac{1}{2}$	10	$10\frac{1}{2}$
British	8	$8\frac{1}{2}$	9	$9\frac{1}{2}$	10	$10\frac{1}{2}$
Continental	0	1	2	3	4	5

(But many European countries use the same as the United States.)

Shoes

U.S.A.	6	$6\frac{1}{2}$	7	$7\frac{1}{2}$	8	$8\frac{1}{2}$
British	$4\frac{1}{2}$	5	$5\frac{1}{2}$	6	$6\frac{1}{2}$	7
Continental	38	38	39	39	40	41

Men

Suits and Overcoats

U.S.A	36	38	40	42	44	46
British	36	38	40	42	44	46
Continental	46	48	50	52	54	56

Shirts

U.S.A.	14½	15	15½	16	16½
European	37	38	39	40	41

Sweaters, T-shirts, and Some Shirts

Small	Sizes under 36 British or U.S.A. or 46 European
Medium	36-38 British or 46-48 European
Large	40 British or European
Extra Large	anything over 40 British or European

Shoes and Slippers

U.S.A.	8	8½	9½	10½	11½	12
British	7	7½	8½	9½	10½	11
European	41	42	43	44	45	46

Americans often use the sizes Small, Medium, Large, or Extra Large.

Translating Cooking Measures

Since recipes and measures will often be given in what will at first be unfamiliar terms, be *sure* to bring your own measuring spoons and cups. Americans rarely use scales in home cooking. The following may be helpful.

1 teaspoon = ⅓ tablespoon

3 teaspoons = 1 tablespoon

2 tablespoons = 1 fluid ounce

4 tablespoons = ¼ cup

8 tablespoons = ½ cup

16 tablespoons = 8 fluid ounces = $^1/_2$ pint = 1 cup

2 cups = 16 fluid ounces = 1 pint = 1 pound

2 pints = 1 quart

4 quarts, liquid = 1 gallon, liquid

8 quarts = 1 peck (dry measure)

Metric Measure by Weight

1 ounce = 30 grams

16 ounces = 1 pound = 454 grams

2 pounds and 3 ounces = 1 kilogram or kilo

14 pounds = 1 stone = 6.36 kilograms

100 grams = 3.5 ounces

200 grams = 7 ounces

400 grams = 14 ounces

454 grams = 16 ounces = 1 pound

Metric Measure by Fluid Volume

1 dram = $^3/_4$ teaspoon = $^1/_8$ ounce = 3.7 milliliters

1 teaspoon = $^1/_6$ ounce = 5 milliliters

1 tablespoon = $^1/_2$ ounce = 15 milliliters

8 tablespoons = $^1/_2$ cup

16 tablespoons = 1 cup = 236 milliliters = .236 liters ($^1/_4$ liter, approx.)

4 cups = 1 quart = .946 liters (1 liter, approx.)

1 milliliter = $^1/_5$ teaspoon

1 liter = 1.057 quarts

4 liters = 1 gallon plus 1 cup

Oven Settings

American Oven Degrees Fahrenheit	Degrees Celsius
140°-250° Low or "Slow"	70°-121°
300°-400° Moderate	150°-205°
400° up High or "Hot"	205° up

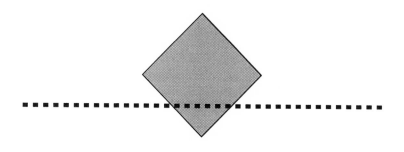

Index